Games for Language Learning

Andrew Wright
David Betteridge and
Michael Buckby

Cambridge University Press
Cambridge
London · New York · Melbourne

Published by the Syndics of the Cambridge University Press
The Pitt Building, Trumpington Street, Cambridge CB2 1RP
Bentley House, 200 Euston Road, London NW1 2DB
32 East 57th Street, New York, NY 10022, U.S.A.
296 Beaconsfield Parade, Middle Park, Melbourne 3206, Australia

© Cambridge University Press 1979

First published 1979

Filmset by Keyspools Ltd., Golborne, Lancs.
Printed in Great Britain at the
University Press, Cambridge

Library of Congress cataloguing in publication data

Wright, Andrew
Games for language learning.

Includes index.

1. Languages, Modern–Study and teaching.
2. Games. I. Betteridge, David, joint author.
II. Buckby, Michael, joint author. III. Title.
PB35.W7   418'.007   79–12274
ISBN 0 521 22170 6

Contents

Acknowledgements

We should like to acknowledge the contributions of teachers and students in many countries who have contributed both ideas and suggestions for improvement to the games described in this book. We should also like to acknowledge our debt to Donn Byrne, Jim Kerr, Alan Maley and the British Council, English Language Teaching Institute, London.

Drawings by Andrew Wright.

Introduction

The index (pages 104–6) will help you find the game you need. The index is divided into three parts:

Language (adjectives, adverbs, nouns, questions, etc.)
Topics (actions, age, character, colours, etc.)
Types of communication (asking questions, giving reasons, comparing, correcting, etc.)

In the body of the book the games are grouped according to their general character and spirit (True/false games, Guessing games, Memory games, etc.). This grouping makes it clear that there are many different versions of each general type of game and that each version may give rise to different language and skills and be appropriate for different levels of language achievement.

We hope that this method of grouping according to types of game will help teachers develop their own games and discover new ones.

Why games?

Language learning is hard work. One must make an effort to understand, to repeat accurately, to manipulate newly understood language and to use the whole range of known language in conversation or written composition. Effort is required at every moment and must be sustained for several years. Games help and encourage many learners to make and sustain these efforts.

Games also help the teacher to create contexts in which the language is useful and meaningful. The learners *want* to take part and in order to do so must understand what others are saying or have written, and they must speak or write in order to express their own point of view.

Many games cause as much density of practice as more conventional drill exercises; some do not. What matters, however, is the *quality* of practice. Learners are more likely to experience the meaning of the language when using it in a game

I

than they are when manipulating it in a conventional drill. Dense practice in exercises which bore or even depress learners is not productive if they 'drop out' before a reasonable level of achievement has been reached.

The need for meaningfulness in language has been accepted for some years. A useful interpretation of 'meaningfulness' is that the learners respond to the content in a positive way. If they are amused, angered, challenged, intrigued or surprised the content is clearly meaningful to them. Thus the meaning of the language they listen to, read, speak and write will be more vividly experienced and, therefore, better remembered.

If it is accepted that games can provide intense and meaningful practice of language then they must be regarded as *central* to a teacher's repertoire. They are thus not for use solely on wet days and at the end of term!

What contribution can games make?

Games can be found to give practice in all the skills (reading, writing, listening and speaking), in all the stages of the teaching/learning sequence (presentation, repetition, recombination, composition) and for many situations and types of communication.

Which age group are games for?

Enjoyment of games is not restricted by age. Some individuals, regardless of age, may be less fond of games than others. But so much depends on the appropriateness of the games and the role of the player.

It is generally accepted that young learners and adults are very willing to play games. (This partly depends on the learners' socio-cultural background.) Early teenagers tend to be more self-conscious and one must take into account their reticence when selecting games for them. Games which can be played in pairs or groups may be particularly useful in this case. It is clear to all observers of classroom practice that the teacher's own belief in the usefulness and appropriateness of a game affects the learners' response. We have observed games and materials normally used in primary schools being accepted by businessmen owing to the conviction of the teacher!

Which level?

Many of the games in this book can, with minor adaptations, be used by beginners and advanced students. However, some of the variations described are for specific levels of ability and achievement.

It is important to note that the most advanced and dedicated students can enjoy and value games if the content and language used are relevant to them.

How to use games

If the teacher is unfamiliar with the variety and use of language teaching games then it is advisable to introduce them slowly as supplementary activities to whatever course book is used. Once the teacher is familiar with a variety of games they can be used as a substitute for parts of the course which the teacher judges to be unsuitable. This book is a resource for the teacher, however, not a course in itself!

It is essential to choose games which are appropriate to the class in terms of language and type of participation. Having chosen an appropriate game, its character and the aims and rules must be made clear to the learners. It may be necessary to use the mother tongue to do this. If the learners are unclear about what they have to do, chaos and disillusionment may result. Many teachers believe that competition should be avoided. It is possible to play the majority of the games in this book with a spirit of challenge to achieve, rather than to 'do someone else down'. We believe that it is wrong and counter-productive to match learners of unequal ability even within a single exchange or challenge. The less able learner may 'give up' and the more able develop a false sense of his or her own achievement. We also believe it is wrong to compel an individual to participate. For many such learners there will be a point of 'readiness to participate' similar to the state of 'reading readiness' in young children. Learners reluctant to participate might be asked to act as judges and scorers.

As with all events in the classroom it is advisable to stop a game and change to something else before the learners become tired of it. In this way their goodwill and concentration are retained.

Class, individual, pair and group work

The notes on each game suggest which form of class organisation is appropriate. Of the four types of grouping the last two are very important if each learner is to have sufficient oral practice in the use of the language. In class work it is easy to demonstrate that learners say only one or two sentences in a lesson or, indeed, in a week. The greatest 'mistake' (if oral ability is an aim) is for the learner not to speak at all! Thus, although some mistakes of grammar or pronunciation or idiom may be made in pair or group work the price is worth paying. If the learners are clear about what they have to do and the language is not beyond them there need be few mistakes.

Pair work: This is easy and fast to organise. It provides opportunities for intensive listening and speaking practice. Pair work is better than group and class work for the shy learner and is better than group work if there are discipline problems. Indeed, for all these reasons we prefer to organise games in pair or general class work, rather than in group work.

Group work: Some games *require* 4–6 players: in these cases group work is essential. Membership of groups should be constant for the sake of goodwill and efficiency. If there is to be competition between groups, they should be of mixed ability. If there is to be no such competition the teacher might choose groups according to ability: this is very much a personal choice.

Many teachers consider it advisable to have a group leader. However, once more, it is our experience that groups can operate perfectly well without a group leader. The leader would normally be one of the more able learners. However, there is much to be said for encouraging a reticent learner by giving the responsibility to him or her. The leader's role is to ensure that the game or activity is properly organised and to act as an intermediary between learners and teacher.

The teacher's role, once the groups are in action, is to go from group to group listening in, contributing and, *if necessary*, correcting.

If a teacher has not organised group work before, then it is advisable to work slowly towards it. First of all, make the learners familiar with work in pairs. Add to this games in which rows of learners (if that is how they are seated) compete against you or between themselves. Finally, after perhaps several weeks, ask the rows of pupils to group themselves together to play a game between themselves.

It is absolutely essential that the learners are totally familiar with the games they are asked to play. (It is helpful if they are familiar with the games in their own language.)

Once the learners are familiar with group work, new games are normally introduced in the following way:

- explanation by the teacher to the class;
- demonstration of parts of the game by the teacher and one or
  two learners;
- trial by a group in front of the class;
- any key language and/or instructions written on the
  blackboard;
- first try by groups;
- key language, etc. removed from the blackboard.

The spirit of real games

Our aim has been to find games which the learners would enjoy
playing in their out-of-classroom lives. Of course, experience of
teaching foreign languages shows that many learners *are* prepared
to take part in games and activities which they would consider a
little juvenile or rather boring in the mother tongue. However,
there is a limit to learners' goodwill and we should not stray far
from the aim of introducing games worth playing in their own
right. It is often the activity expected of a learner which makes it
into an acceptable game, or, on the other hand, into a mechanical
exercise. One example of this must suffice:

The teacher places a number of pens, pencils, etc. in various
places on his desk. He asks a learner, for example, 'Where's the red
pen?' As the red pen is obviously on the book, the learner
understands the question as, 'What sentence in English describes the
position of the pen?'

However, if the teacher says, 'Look carefully at the pens,
pencils, etc. Now turn round. Where's the red pen? Can you
remember?' In this case the learner's powers of memory are
challenged and he or she is motivated to think or speak. And,
most importantly, he or she understands the question in the same
way as a native speaker.

Collecting new games

Any games or activities which involve language and which your
learners enjoy are language learning material. You can find 'new'
games by studying magazines, newspapers, radio and television
programmes, party games and indeed by asking your learners. If
you can create these games in the classroom and the language is
appropriate, then they are useful.

It is usually difficult to find a new game for specific language
practice just when you need it. It is a wise precaution to collect

and file games for use whenever you happen to come across them. Games without materials can be described as in this book and filed in a ring binder. Games with visual materials could be kept in similar sized envelopes bound in the same folder. It is helpful if the description of the game is written on the outside of the envelope and the visuals and handouts kept inside.

When collecting games it is important to note what language need only be understood by the players and what language must be used by them. (Indeed, in some games the learners are only expected to listen, understand, and, for example, point to a picture or carry out an action.) Thus, the language level is determined by the type of use, not just the structures and vocabulary items themselves.

Language for the organisation of games

1   General commands, instructions, etc.

Take your time.
Don't be in such a hurry.
Look.
Turn round.
Stand in a line.
In twos.
One at a time.

PUPIL'S LANGUAGE

Hurry up.
Be quiet.
Be careful.

2   Organisation

a) Things required for the lesson

TEACHER'S LANGUAGE

John,	could you	give out	the pencils,	please?
	would you		the scissors,	
	will you		the rulers,	

Fetch	the tape recorder	from the storeroom, will you?
	the projector	

Bring	me	some chalk,	please.
Give		some paper,	
		a pencil,	

You need pencils, rulers, scissors . . .
You'll need . . .
You'll all need . . .
You each need a pencil, a ruler, scissors . . .

7

You'll each need . . .
Have you got pencils, rulers, scissors?
Have you all got . . . ?
Have you each got a pencil, a ruler, scissors . . . ?

Put up your hand(s) | if you need anything.
                      | if you haven't got anything.

What | do you need?
       | haven't you got?

Look. | There's one here.
      | There are some over there.

Here you are. Come and get | it.
                          | them.
                          | some.

Help | yourself.
     | yourselves.

One for you, and one for you . . .
One | each.
Two
Three
Four

One between | two.
             | three.
             | four.

One | for each group.
Two
Three

You'll have to share.
Who can lend John a pencil?

Please, | may | I | give out | the | pencils?
       | could | | fetch | | scissors?
       | can | | | | rulers?

I'm sorry, I can't find | the pencils.
                          | the scissors.
                          | the rulers.
                          | them.
                          | any.

I haven't got	a pencil.
	one.
	any.

Please may I have . . . ?
(I'm sorry, but) my pencil's broken.

Look.	There's one	over there.
	There it is	on the table.
	There are some	on the desk.
	There they are	by the window.

Here you are.
One for you, and one for you . . .

b) Arrangement of the classroom

TEACHER'S LANGUAGE

Move	the	desk(s)	over there, please.
Put	your	chair(s)	
Take		things	

Move	the	desk(s)	back where	it	came from.
Put	your	chair(s)		they	
Take		things			

c) Grouping of pupils

TEACHER'S LANGUAGE

Work with the person sitting next to you.

Work in	twos.
	threes.
	fours.
	your groups.

Split	into your groups (now), please.
Go	
Get	

John, (would you) sit	next to	Peter, please(?)
	behind	
	in front of	

In groups. In your groups.
On your own. By yourself.
You be the group leader.
Would you be the group leader?

Who's next? Whose turn is it?

PUPIL'S LANGUAGE

| I want | to work with ... |
| I'd like | |

Let me	have a	turn.
Let's		go.
		look.

I	haven't had a	turn	(yet).
We		go	
		look	

| Whose | turn | is it? |
| | go | |

| You do it | first. |
| | next. |

| Let me | do it | first. |
| Let's | | next. |

d) Organisation of the game

TEACHER'S LANGUAGE

First,	...
Then,	
Next,	
Finally,	

It's your turn. Is it your turn?
It'll be your turn next.
Who hasn't had a turn yet?
You take it in turns.

3 Other activities

TEACHER'S LANGUAGE

If you want any help, put up your hand(s).

| Who wants to | try? |
| | have a go? |

You must ...
You've got to ...

When he . . . then you must . . .
You take it in turns.

4 Praise, blame, and evaluation

TEACHER'S LANGUAGE

(I think) | this one | is | better than | that one.
| these | are | | those.

I don't think | this one | is | as good as | that one.
| these | are | | those.

Good. Quite good. Very good. O.K. Fine. Great.
Well done. Good | boy. | Right. Correct.
| girl. |

Wrong. Not right. Not very good.
Not quite right.

PUPIL'S LANGUAGE

Is | it | all right?
| this |

(I think) | it's good.
| that's poor.
| this is great.
| they're rubbish.

5 Interpersonal exchanges

TEACHER'S LANGUAGE
What's wrong? Can I help you?
All right?

PUPIL'S LANGUAGE

Please,   Mr Smith,   . . .
Excuse me, Mrs Smith,
           Miss Smith,
           Dr Smith,
           Sir,
           Miss,

Would you like to . . .?
Let's . . .

Yes. No. O.K. All right. Certainly not.
Of course.
Wait a moment. Hurry up.
I've finished.

True/false games

1 Repeat it if it's true

Language, topic, type of communication Repeating sentences after the teacher. Distinguishing true and false statements.

Skills Listening and speaking

Degree of control Teacher-controlled

Level Beginners

Time 5–10 minutes

Preparation About 10–15 pictures which you can hold up and which may be seen the length of the classroom. Each picture should emphasise a single concept, e.g.
running, swimming, climbing
has got . . . hasn't got . . .
some, any
in, on, under, next to

Procedure Class work

Hold up one of the pictures and make a true *or* false statement about it. The class should listen and repeat what you have said, *if it is true*.
You can have a competition with the class. Give yourself a point every time you can get the class to repeat something which is untrue, and give the class a point when they respond correctly (by repeating something true or ignoring something false).
Teacher: He's running.
Class: He's running.
Teacher: That's one point for you.

Teacher: She's swimming.
Class:
Teacher: That's another point for you.

2 Correct me if I'm wrong

Language, topic, type of communication Identifying mistakes, correcting mistakes, and interrupting politely, using *Excuse me, you said . . ., You should have said . . . instead.*

Skills Listening, speaking and reading

Degree of control Guided

Level All

Time 10 minutes

Preparation Any text which all the learners can have copies of.

Procedure Class, group or pair work

Read out the text and deliberately change some of it.
The learners should follow their copy of the text and immediately stop you when they notice one of the changes.
Once the game is understood it can be played in groups or pairs, e.g. one might read the text as, 'Read out the text and deliberately change all of it. The learners must follow . . .'
Learner: Excuse me, you said 'all' instead of 'some' and you should have said, 'The learners should follow'.

3 Don't let them pull your leg

Language, topic, type of communication Making sentences, first in the affirmative then in the negative (*'s not, don't,* etc.)

Skills Principally listening for detail. Speaking and writing occur in group or pair work.

Degree of control Free

Level All

Time 15–20 minutes to prepare a text. 3–4 minutes for each learner who reads a text.

Preparation None, unless you would like to prepare your talk: see Procedure below.

Procedure   Class, group or pair work

Discuss the idea that there are always people who like 'to pull other people's legs', i.e. to make them look a little foolish. Explain that this game will train the learners not to have their legs pulled! Explain that you will talk and include a few untrue statements. The learners must immediately raise their hands on hearing an untrue statement and say what is wrong with it.

Once the idea of the game is understood, it can be played in groups or in pairs. Learners might prepare their 'talk' in writing, perhaps for homework.

Teacher *or* Learner 1:	Yesterday I went into town and saw a marvellous car. It had six legs and went very . . .
Learner 2:	That's not true. Cars don't have legs, they have wheels. And they don't have *six* wheels either.
Teacher:	Oh, sorry. You are quite right. Anyway, it was going very fast indeed. I was at the chemist's buying some bread . . .
Teacher:	Paris is the capital of Italy . . .
Learner 3:	*Rome* is the capital of Italy!

Guessing games

4 Hiding and finding

Language, topic, type of communication — Asking questions, using *Is it* + preposition + place (e.g. *Is it on top of the cupboard?*) Making suggestions, using *Let's* + verb + object + preposition + place (e.g. *Let's hide the watch on top of the cupboard*).
In Variation 1: Have you hidden it . . .?
In Variation 2: Is it hidden . . .?
or Has it been hidden . . .?

Skills — Listening and speaking

Degree of control — Guided

Level — Beginners, and in Variations 1 and 2, intermediate

Time — 15 minutes

Preparation — None

Procedure — Class work

One or two learners should be sent outside the room. The class then discuss what small object they would like to hide and where it should be hidden, e.g.
Class: Let's hide this watch.
       Let's hide this coin.

       Let's hide it under the box of chalk.
       Let's hide it inside the cupboard on a shelf.

When the object is hidden, call the learner(s) in and tell him/them to find the object by asking questions, e.g.
Learner 1: Is it at the front of the room?
Class: Yes.
Learner 1: Is it on top of the cupboard?
Class: No . . .

Variation 1 — At an intermediate level, the learner(s) who went outside the classroom can be asked to use the present perfect:

Learner 1: Have you hidden it near the door?

Variation 2 One or two learners go out of the classroom but only *half* the class should be responsible for choosing and hiding the object. This gives some justification for the use of the passive form if it is the *other* half of the class which is asked the questions:
Learner 1: Is it hidden at the back of the classroom?
      or Has it been hidden at the back of the classroom?

5 Box

Language, topic, Naming and describing objects, identifying objects from their
type of descriptions, using nouns (e.g. comb, watch), adjectives (e.g.
communication silver), possessives (e.g. my, mine, John's). In the Variation, *Have you got a . . .?* is used.

Skills Listening and speaking

Degree of control Free

Level All

Time 5 minutes

Preparation Any large box or bag. Ensure that a variety of small objects which the learners can name are in the classroom. You could keep small objects in your pocket and use that instead of a box or bag.

Procedure Class work

Go round the classroom picking up about ten small objects. Ask the learners to name each object before you put it into the box or bag.
Put your hand into the box, take hold of one of the objects but do not take it out.
Teacher: What have I got in my hand?
Learner 1: A comb.
      or The comb.
Teacher: No.
Learner 2: A watch.
      or The watch.
Teacher: Yes.

At this point, walk towards the learner who has guessed correctly to give him or her the object. If any other learner can say anything true about the object, he or she must call it out immediately. Walk towards that learner to give him or her the object. Again, other learners may attempt to 'win' the object by calling out a true statement.

Learner 3: It's a silver watch.
Learner 4: It's fast.
Learner 5: It's ticking.
Learner 6: It's not Big Ben.
Learner 7: It's like a person. It has a face and two hands.

When the game is over, make use of possessive forms in returning the objects to their owners.
Teacher: Whose is this?
Learner: It's mine/his/John's, etc.

Variation	The learners may guess what is in the box by asking the question 'Have you got a . . . ?'

6   What on earth is he talking about?

Language, topic, type of communication	Describing things, people, settings and their relationships, using any appropriate complete sentence.
Skills	Listening, speaking, reading and writing
Degree of control	Free
Level	All
Time	10–20 minutes for written preparation. 5–10 minutes for listening and speaking in pairs.
Preparation	Prepare one or two descriptions as examples for the learners (see below).
Procedure	Class work, leading to group or pair work

Demonstrate the game yourself. Think of an object which may be in the room, or in a picture on the wall, and describe it. Tell the learners to raise their hands if they think they know what you are describing. Finally, see who has guessed correctly.
Then tell everyone to prepare a description in writing of any object; this might be done for homework.
It may help to write down on the blackboard examples of the language items the learners will need, e.g.

It's . . . (colour)
It's . . . (size)
It's . . . (shape)
It's made of . . . (substance)
It's used for . . . (purpose)
It belongs to . . . (owner)

For beginners, you might restrict the choice to common objects.
For intermediate and advanced students more bizarre objects, or
actions or abstract concepts might be chosen.

Memory games

7 What's behind you?

Language, topic, type of communication
Listing and describing objects and places, and, in Variations 1 and 2, describing people's appearance, e.g. *There's a . . ., There are some . . ., There aren't any . . ., He/She's wearing . . .*

Skills
Listening and speaking

Degree of control
Free

Level
Beginners/intermediate

Time
2–3 minutes

Preparation
None

Procedure
Class work

Tell the class not to turn round. Ask them what they think is behind them. They might list other people in the class, furniture, pictures on the walls, windows, etc. Ask for descriptions of the things they mention. You might also ask what the learners can remember of the street outside the school, e.g.

Teacher: Think about the street outside the school. What can you remember?
Learner 1: There are some trees . . .
Teacher: Yes. Are there trees on *both* sides of the street?
Learner 1: No, there aren't any on the other side.
Learner 2: No! There's one by the grocer's.

Variation 1
Before you explain the game to the class, ask two of them to go outside the classroom. Explain the game and ask the learners to describe what the two are wearing. You could write on the board a summary of what they say. Ask the two outside to come back in and compare.

Variation 2
A learner is asked to close his eyes and describe his neighbour's appearance.

8 Kim's game

Language, topic, type of communication	Listing and naming objects, or pictures of objects. Variation 1: Numbers and plurals (e.g. *Three suitcases*) Variation 2: Adjectives (e.g. *A red suitcase . . . The green case is bigger . . .*) Variation 3: Containers (e.g. *A bottle of milk*) Variation 4: Present perfect (*You've put . . .*), past simple (*It was . . .*) and prepositions (e.g. *next to . . .*) Variation 6: Present perfect and comparatives (e.g. *You've made the tree taller.*) Variation 6: Describing and comparing
Skills	Listening, speaking and writing
Degree of control	Guided
Level	Beginners/intermediate
Time	5 minutes
Preparation	Make a collection of small objects or pictures of objects which you know the learners can name. If you want to display the objects and/or pictures on a table, make sure in advance that all the learners can see. If they cannot see the table clearly, then you must use the pictures only and display them on a board. Have a cloth or sheet of paper ready to hide the objects and/or pictures. Each learner will need a pencil and paper.
Procedure	Class work, leading to optional pair work. Lay 6–8 objects and/or pictures on the table, or display 6–8 pictures on the board. Tell the learners that you are going to challenge their powers of observation and memory. Give the learners 20 seconds to look at the objects and/or pictures, then hide them with a cloth or sheet of paper. Tell the learners to write down as many names as they can remember. Then ask them to tell you what they have written. Teacher: What have you written? *or* What can you remember? Finally, remove the cloth or sheet of paper and let the learners compare their lists with the objects and/or pictures.
Warning	Make sure that everyone can see the objects and/or pictures.

Variation 1   *Numbers and plurals*
If you want the learners to practise numbers and plural forms, then make sure you have several objects and/or pictures which are the same, for example three suitcases, two cameras and one typewriter.

Variation 2   *Adjectives*
To enable the learners to use adjectives, have several objects and/or pictures which are of the same kind but are of different colour, size, shape, etc. For example, include a red, a black and a green suitcase. This can give excellent practice in the use of comparatives, e.g. 'The green case is a bit bigger than the black case and it's about the same size as the red case'.

Variation 3   *Containers*
Use, for example, a bottle of milk, a box of matches, a tin of soup, a packet of soap powder, a bag of apples and a tube of toothpaste.

Variation 4   *Present perfect, past simple, prepositions*
This variation of the game usually works better with real objects than with pictures. Remember that 'real' objects may include toys, such as a plane, car or bridge. Place 6–8 objects on a table. Make sure that several of them are positioned, for example, on top of/underneath/next to/inside other objects.
After 20 seconds, ask the learners to look away. Change the position of one of the objects.
Teacher: What have I done?
Learner: You've put the tape underneath the dictionary.
Teacher: And where was it?
Learner: It was next to the watch.

Variation 5   *Comparatives and present perfect*
Instead of using objects or prepared pictures ask a number of learners to draw some simple objects on the OHP or the board. (This in itself will provide a rich language situation!) Some of the objects might have colour on them.
Tell the learners to close their eyes and to put their heads on their arms whilst you, or a learner, *change* some of the drawings making them longer or shorter, fatter, taller, redder, greener, etc.
Challenge the class to tell you what you have done, e.g.
Teacher: What have I done?
Learner: You've made the tree taller.
    or   The tree is taller.
The learners can play the same game in pairs using paper, pencil and rubber.

Variation 6   *Describing and comparing*
For more advanced students, you may show them about 15
objects or pictures of objects and then ask them to write down
what they remember, *describing the objects* in detail. It is easier and
equally challenging to show the objects or pictures *one after the
other* instead of at the same time.
When the learners have written down everything they can
remember, they should exchange their writing with their
neighbours. Each learner marks his neighbour's work as you hold
up the objects and pictures again.
As you hold up each object, discuss with the class its character, e.g.

Teacher: What's this?
Learner 1:   A scarf.
Teacher: Did John remember it?
Learner 1:   Yes, he did.
Teacher: What did he say about it?
             How did he describe it?
Learner 1:   He said (reading from his partner's work) it was red,
             green, yellow . . . and woolly.
Teacher: Well! Is it? Was he right?
Learner 2:   No, he wasn't.
             It isn't red, it's orange!
Teacher: Well, it's sort of red, isn't it?
Learner 3:   And it isn't green.
Teacher: Tell me when John was right and when he was wrong.
Learner 4:   He was right when he said that the scarf is (was) red,
             yellow and woolly, and wrong when he said that it is
             (was) green.

9   Pass the message

Language, topic,   Repeating whole sentences.
type of
communication

Skills   Listening, speaking, reading and writing

Degree of control   Teacher-controlled, and, for advanced students, free

Level   All

Time   10–15 minutes for the discussion at the end of the game, or longer
with advanced students. The game itself can be played while other
work is going on.

23

Memory games

Preparation Prepare a message before the lesson. Here are some examples for different levels of learners, e.g.

57394

My black, heavy bag is under the bush.

I will be waiting for you just outside the swing doors of the Green Pig at a quarter to nine.

Each learner should have a pen and a piece of paper.

You might first consider discussing the prevalent and destructive nature of rumour with the class. Then introduce this game as an example of how difficult it is to report things accurately.

Procedure Class work

Show the sentence you have prepared to someone sitting at the front and to one side. Let this player see the sentence for 5 seconds, then take it from him and keep it yourself. That first player must then write the sentence he remembers on a piece of paper and show it to his neighbour for 5 seconds. The neighbour does the same until the message, usually much changed, has gone round the class.

Throughout this part of the game you can carry on with your normal lesson.

When you see that the message has reached the last person, ask him to read out what he has written down.

There will probably be cries of astonishment!

Then read out the message as it began.

Now ask all the learners in turn to read out the message *they* passed on.

If you want to get some intensive language work out of the game, particularly for the advanced students, discuss why each of the changes might have been made. Are they changes which don't change the sense significantly? Are the changes grammatically wrong? Making a detailed analysis of these changes can be a very subtle and informative activity.

Variation 1 More stress can be given to listening and speaking if the message is *whispered* to the neighbour. This can be done as a race. Different teams 'pass' the same message which you whisper to the learners at the front of each team or row. The player at the end acts appropriately, e.g.

Open a window, please.

Please give me a black pencil.

Would you please draw a square on the blackboard.

Variation 2 Instead of attempting to pass on the message received, each player should deliberately distort it in some way with the aim of creating an outrageous rumour. Otherwise the same procedure applies as above.

Variation 3   A short story or joke is whispered, not just a sentence.

10   Pelmanism

Language, topic, type of communication   Making comments about the Pelmanism cards provided, and agreeing and disagreeing politely (e.g. *I'm sorry I don't . . .*). In Variation 2, the learners use *I've got . . . have you got . . .? What have you got . . .?*

Skills   Listening, speaking and reading

Degree of control   Guided

Level   All learners will enjoy playing this game, although Variation 2 is most useful for beginners/intermediate learners.

Time   10–15 minutes, except for Variation 2, which takes 5–10 minutes.

Preparation   Prepare a set of 20 matching cards for each group of 4–5 players. Alternatively, the learners can produce the cards.
In each set, there are 10 pairs of cards: the pairs can relate to each other in a range of ways, according to the language needs of the learners, e.g.
On one card the picture of an invention and on the other the date it was invented.
On one card a photo (from a magazine) of a person, object or scene and on the other a written description of it.
On one card is written a statement and an invitation to the learner to find a response which he could use to agree, disagree politely, partly agree, etc.; on the other card is the response he needs.

Procedure   Group work

The learners, in groups of 4–5, lay the cards in neat rows face down so that the pictures and writing on the cards cannot be seen. One player then picks up two of the cards. If he thinks they match, he makes some appropriate comment to the others, e.g.
Aspirin was invented in 1853.
This car is green and it is made in France.
To disagree politely a learner could say, 'I'm sorry I don't agree

with that. I think that . . .'
If the other players agree, he keeps the two cards and can pick up
two more.
When two cards are picked up which do not match, they must be
shown to the other players and replaced in exactly the same
position from which they were taken. Then the next player has a
turn.
This continues until all the cards have been paired off. The player
with the most pairs is the winner.
Further examples for the cards:
words and their definitions
maps of countries (from travel brochures) and the name of the
    country
coins or stamps and the name of their country of origin
titles of books or quotations and their authors
pictures of different fish, trees, birds, flowers, etc. and their names
photographs and matching dialogues
cartoons and their captions (cut from comics, etc.)
riddles and their solutions
questions and answers

Variation 1   To allow the learners to become accustomed to the cards and thus
reduce the chances of too much argument later, they could play
with the cards individually, or in pairs, before using them to play
Pelmanism. They could time themselves to see how quickly they
match all the cards.
This is particularly beneficial as a means of keeping usefully
occupied those learners who finish a piece of work before the
others.
It is a good idea to keep sets of these cards always available for
such situations.

Variation 2   Give one card to each player. The players then look at their cards
and try to find who has the matching card by asking other
learners, e.g.
I've got a picture of the Canadian flag. What have you got?
Have you got the card that goes with this?

Question and answer games

11 Don't say 'Yes' or 'No'

Language, topic,
type of
communication
Asking questions and giving answers, especially asking questions with question tags (e.g. . . ., *isn't it? . . ., don't you? . . ., do you?*) and giving complete phrases for answers.
Using *of course, of course not, perhaps, clearly, obviously, I'm sure, I've no idea.*

Skills Listening and speaking

Degree of control Guided

Level Intermediate/advanced

Time 5–10 minutes

Preparation None

Procedure Class work, leading to group or pair work

This can be a team competition. Put a number of questions to each team. Each question must be answered without delay and without the use of either 'Yes. or 'No'. The team which answers the most questions in this way wins.
The teacher asks questions of this type:
Your name is Peter, isn't it?
You do live near the school, don't you?
You don't come to school by bus, do you?
You didn't do your homework last night, did you?
It was raining at 9 o'clock this morning, wasn't it?
The learners should reply, e.g.
Not at all, my name is Ann.
Not quite, my home is a long way from school.
Indeed I do.
I certainly did.
I don't think so.
When the learners have seen how the game works, they can fire questions at each other to try to catch each other out.

Warning   Make sure that the learners are already familiar with the more usual responses beginning with 'Yes' or 'No'. Of course, the learners should also be clear about the various alternative responses. These might be written on the board.

12   Half the class knows

Language, topic,   Asking questions and giving answers, with expressions such as *not*
type of   *exactly . . .*
communication

Skills   Listening and speaking

Degree of control   Free

Level   All

Time   5–10 minutes

Preparation   For class work you should have 3–6 pictures of magazine page size. They should not be too detailed. Stickmen drawings are ideal but simple photographs are also suitable. See examples opposite. For pair or group work you will need 3–6 pictures for each pair or group.

Procedure   Class work leading to group or pair work

You or a learner or a group of learners look at a picture which the rest of the class cannot see. (This is an opportunity to involve a less able learner in a key role.) The ones who cannot see must ask questions to find out what is in the picture.
The game may be played at a variety of levels. At the simplest level, you may say there is a man in the picture and ask, e.g.
Teacher: What is he doing?
Class: Is he running?
Teacher: No.
Class: Is he swimming?

At a more advanced level, you may use a more complicated picture and give no clue concerning the content of it, e.g.
Class: Is it inside?
Teacher: No, not exactly.
Class: Outside?
Teacher: Well . . . yes, but partly inside.
Class: Is it a door?

13 Test your knowledge

Language, topic, type of communication	Any questions of fact, and answers to them.
Skills	Reading
Degree of control	Teacher-controlled
Level	Intermediate/advanced
Time	10–20 minutes
Preparation	Cut out at least 20 pieces of paper or card, about 5cm × 10cm. Dividing these into pairs, write a question on one of the cards and the appropriate answer on the other. (The learners themselves could be asked to do this.) Here are three types of subject with a few examples:

General knowledge

Where is the Taj Mahal?	It's in India.
Where was Tolstoy born?	In Russia.
What is the capital of Scotland?	Edinburgh.
How many players are there in a cricket team?	Eleven.
Who painted 'Guernica'?	Picasso.

Jokes

Which king of England wore the largest shoes?	The one with the largest feet.
What can you have when someone has taken it?	A photograph.
What is the difference between a nail and a bad boxer?	One is knocked in, the other is knocked out.
Waiter, there is a dead fly in my soup!	Yes, sir, it's the hot water which has killed it.

Cause and effect

What would happen if the sun lost its heat?	All living things would die.
What would happen if we didn't eat for a long time?	We would die.

	What happens when we add blue to yellow?	It turns green.
	What happens if we boil an egg for six minutes?	It becomes hard.
Procedure	Pair/individual work	

Explain that the questions must be paired with the appropriate answers.

Variation   Sentences are divided into two parts. Each part is written on a separate card. Learners must sort out the cards and put the correct pairs together.

14   Twenty questions

Language, topic, type of communication   Asking questions to acquire information.

Skills   Listening and speaking

Degree of control   Free

Level   Intermediate/advanced

Time   15 minutes

Preparation   None

Procedure   Class work

There are many versions of this game. A common version is played regularly on BBC radio. In this, the question-master thinks of something and simply tells the players whether it is 'animal, vegetable, mineral or abstract'. The players can then put 20 questions to the question-master to discover what he is thinking of. Traditionally, the questions are put so that they can be answered by 'Yes' or 'No'. The teacher may, of course, limit the choice, for example, to everyday objects, pets, professions, verbs, phrases, famous people and where they live.
If a learner acts as the question-master, you have the opportunity of helping the class by asking a few questions which narrow down the range of possibilities, e.g.
Is it bigger/smaller than a car?
Can you eat it?

Have you got one?
Would you normally find one in a house?
Is it made of wood?
Can it be easily broken?
If the players discover what it is in less than 20 questions, they win a point. If they do not, the question-master scores a point.

Variation 1   You can give part of a simple story to the class and they can try to find out more, or complete the story, in 20 questions.

Variation 2   The teacher, or a learner, pretends that he is a famous person, dead or alive, or that he lives in a well-known city. The players can ask 20 questions to try to discover who, or where, the questioner is.

Variation 3   A learner thinks of a profession and writes it down. The class have twenty questions to find the answer.

Variation 4   A learner says, 'I've got an interesting pet' and the others ask, 'Has it got four legs?', 'Can it fly?' etc., until the correct answer is guessed. If a learner receives the answer 'yes', he is allowed a further question.

Variation 5   A learner thinks of a verb or verb phrase, e.g. 'sing', 'play football', which he writes down or whispers to the teacher. The others then ask, 'Do you "coffee pot"★ at home/with your friends/in the bath?' until they guess the answer.
★'Coffee pot' is just a nonsensical idea which is substituted for the missing verb.

15   General knowledge quiz

Language, topic, type of communication   Wh- questions, agreeing, disagreeing, speculating, expressing doubt, ignorance, e.g.
Yes, I think you're right . . .
Would I be right in thinking . . . ?

Skills   Listening and speaking

Degree of control   Free

Level   Intermediate/advanced

Time   10–15 minutes

Preparation   The quiz can cover a range of topics, or can concentrate on one
area. It is important that none of the learners should know the
answers to all the questions, so that the speculation and argument
are real and so that the learners acquire some new information
through the foreign language. An excellent source for such
quizzes is *The Guinness Book of Records*. This may suggest, in
particular, quizzes using superlatives and comparatives. The
following quiz examples would give practice in the use of past
tenses.

1 Who first sailed alone around the world?
   a) Sir Francis Drake
   b) Sir Francis Chichester
   c) *Joshua Slocum, an American*
   d) Christopher Columbus
2 Who first flew alone across the Atlantic?
   a) *Charles Lindberg*
   b) The Wright brothers
   c) Alexander Fleming
   d) Louis Pasteur
3 Who produced the first television picture?
   a) *The Scotsman, John Baird*
   b) The American, Neil Armstrong
   c) The Russian, Yuri Gagarin
   d) The Englishman, George Stephenson

The following examples give practice in the use and
understanding of wh- questions.

1 Where is the Eiffel Tower?
2 Where was Shakespeare born?
3 Who is the American president?
4 Who wrote *Robinson Crusoe*?
5 What are the colours of the British flag?
6 What is the capital of Italy?
7 How many players are there in a football team?
8 How does the petrol engine work?
9 Which is the longest river in the world?
10 In which countries does the elephant live?

Procedure   Class work

When a learner first hazards a guess, e.g. 'Was it Sir Francis Drake
who first sailed alone around the world?' the teacher should
neither confirm nor correct the answer. He should rather use it to
stimulate others to agree or disagree, e.g.
Do you agree with that?
What do you think?

33

Does anyone disagree?
Does everyone agree?
Only after a good deal of discussion should the teacher say which
is the correct answer. He could then use the incorrect answers to
stimulate more discussion, e.g.
What did Sir Francis Drake/Christopher Columbus do?
Why was Louis Pasteur famous?
The teacher can act as a model, reminding the learners of the sorts
of expressions they can use in such a situation, e.g.
Would I be right in thinking that . . . ?
Did he, by any chance . . . ?
Yes, I think you're right when you say . . ., but . . .
No, I don't think that can be right, because . . .

16   What were you doing last night?

Language, topic, type of communication	Asking questions (*Who . . . ? Did . . . ?* etc.)
Skills	Listening and speaking
Degree of control	Free
Level	Intermediate/advanced
Time	10–15 minutes
Preparation	None
Procedure	Class work

Make a statement and explain that the learners should question
you about it, e.g.
Teacher: I saw an old friend last night.
Learner 1:   Where did you see him?
Teacher: He came to my house.
Learner 2:   Did you have dinner?
Teacher: Yes.
Learner 3:   Who cooked the dinner?
Teacher: I did.
Learner 4:   What did you cook?

A more gamelike quality will emerge if you create a fantasy, e.g.
Teacher: I saw a green man last night.

Learner 1: Where?
Teacher: He was on the Underground.
Learner 2: What was he doing?
Teacher: Talking.
Learner: Who was he talking to?
Teacher: A small, silver dog.
Learner: Did he speak in English?
Teacher: Yes.

Other opening statements might be:
My friend has just bought a new car.
My neighbours had a quarrel last night.
My great–grandfather has just had a marvellous holiday.
I've got a wonderful parrot.

Picture games

17 Guess what I'm drawing

Language, topic,
type of
communication

Use of vocabulary items in reply to questions, perhaps in such sentence patterns as *I think it's going to be a . . .* or *It might be a . . .*

Skills   Listening and speaking

Degree of control   Guided

Level   Beginners

Time   5–10 minutes for class work,
10–15 minutes for pair work

Preparation   You need a chalk board or OHP and paper and pencils for each learner.

Procedure   Class work leading to pair work

Start to draw on the board or OHP, asking, e.g.

Teacher: What am I drawing?
Class: A table.
Teacher: No. (continuing to draw)
Class: A house?
Teacher: No, not exactly. (continuing to draw)
Class: A shop.
Teacher: Yes, but what's happening?
Class: There's a tree . . .
Teacher: No.
Class: A fire. The shop is burning!
Teacher: Yes. Now who is this?
Class: The shopkeeper.
Teacher: And what's he doing?

The learners might then play this game in pairs.

18 Copy a picture

Language, topic, type of communication	Correcting, criticising, praising, with use of adjectives, e.g. *It's too . . . It's not . . . enough. That's better.*
Skills	Listening and speaking
Degree of control	Guided
Level	Beginners
Time	10–15 minutes
Preparation	You need a chalk board or OHP and, for pair work, paper, pencils and erasers for everyone.
Procedure	Class work leading to pair work

Draw, or ask a learner to draw, a picture on the board.
See examples on p. 38.

Now ask another learner to draw on the board a copy of the first drawing. As he does so, encourage the class to make helpful comments.
Class: His head is too big.
His legs aren't long enough.
His body is too fat.
The stripes are too narrow.
His trousers are too wide.
His face is too ugly.
That's better.
Good.

Organise pair work in the usual way. Each learner should draw a picture and take it in turns to copy his partner's.

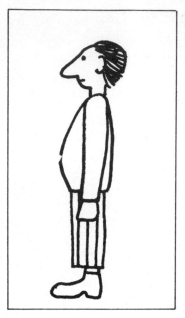

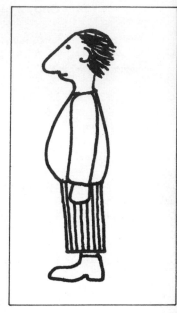

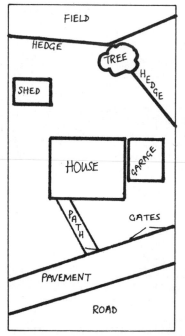

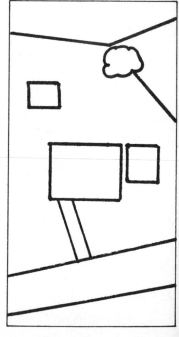

Picture games

19   That's an unusual view!

Language, topic, type of communication	Naming and describing objects (*It's a . . .*) or expressing ignorance (*I don't know* or *I've no idea*). In Variation 1, the phrase *It's part of . . .* is used.
Skills	Listening and speaking
Degree of control	Guided
Level	Beginners
Time	10–15 minutes
Preparation	Prepare a few drawings of unusual views of common objects on sheets of paper or for the OHP.
Procedure	Class work, optionally leading to group work

Draw several examples of unusual views of objects on the board or the OHP. Ask what they are and, once identified, draw or show a picture of the same object from a more familiar angle.
Teacher: What's this?
Learner 1:   It's a woman's face.
Teacher: She hasn't got any eyes or a nose!
Learner 2:   It's a beefburger.
Teacher: Yes. It's a beefburger from above.

Ask the learners to prepare ideas of their own for a few minutes and then to challenge the rest of the class or group. If the learners cannot answer, they must say, 'I don't know' or 'I've no idea'.

Variation 1	Use pictures from magazines, etc. These may be unusual views of objects or parts of objects which you have cut out. If you show parts of objects the learner should say, 'part of', e.g. Learner 1: It's part of a wheel.
Variation 2	Show a small part of a picture as you pull it from an envelope. Let the class guess what it might be.

20   Predicting pictures

Language, topic, type of communication	Future with *going to*. Exclamations of pleasure (e.g. *Marvellous!*) and of regret (e.g. *What a pity!*).

39

Skills	Listening and speaking
Degree of control	Guided
Level	Beginners/intermediate
Time	10–15 minutes
Preparation	Collect 15–20 pictures of objects from a catalogue or magazine. Alternatively you may draw them. (The pictures from 'Happy twins' (Game 21) may be used.)
Procedure	Class, group or pair work

The learners should first familiarise themselves with the pictures on the cards. Then mix all the pictures and lay them in a pile, face down. Players take it in turns to try to predict the next picture: if they are right they take it and if they are wrong they place it at the bottom of the pack, e.g.

Learner 1: It's going to be a typewriter. No! What a pity! (What a shame!) (puts it underneath the pack)

Learner 2: It's going to be a kettle. Yes, it's mine! Marvellous!

21 Happy twins

Language, topic, type of communication	Describing pictures of objects and people.
Skills	Listening and speaking
Degree of control	Free
Level	Intermediate
Time	10–15 minutes
Preparation	Collect 16–20 pictures of single objects or people from magazines, or draw them. Most of the pictures should be of *identical* objects or people. Put all the pictures into an envelope, together with the instructions for the game. Note how many pairs there are. One set of pictures will be needed for each pair of learners.
Procedure	Pair work

The aim is for two players, working together, to collect all the pairs.

The pictures should be mixed and placed in a pile face down.

Each player takes it in turn to pick up a card *without showing it to the other*. Then each player describes his own card *without letting the other see*. The players can also ask each other questions.

If they decide they have a pair, they place them on the table. If the cards *are* a pair they put them on one side. If the cards are not a pair they put them back into the pack.

22 Describe a picture

Language, topic, type of communication — Describing pictures, asking questions, making comparisons, encouraging, praising, criticising.

Skills — Listening and speaking, and, in the Variation, reading and writing

Degree of control — Free

Level — Intermediate/advanced

Time — 15–20 minutes

Preparation — Select from magazines any pictures which show a number of different objects. The objects should be clear in shape and the pictures should preferably not include people. It is amusing if the objects are bizarre in some way – but this is not essential. Alternatively, the language can be limited if the original is a simple line drawing *or* the language may be specialised if the original is a technical diagram.
See examples on p. 42.

For each pair of learners you will need one picture, a piece of paper and a pencil.

Procedure — Pair work

One learner describes the picture to the other who must try to draw it. *The other must not see the original*, e.g.

Learner 1: There is a square table in the picture. It is in the middle of the picture.
Learner 2: About here?
Learner 1: Yes . . . well, a little further down.

Learner 2: Is it like that?
Learner 1: No, not quite, the legs are too long.

When the 'artist' and his 'patron' have done as much as they can, the original and the copy should be compared, e.g.
Learner 2: Oh, the table legs are too long!
Learner 1: I told you they were. But you wouldn't change them!

Variation This variation involves descriptive writing. Each learner is given a picture to describe in writing. When the descriptions are ready, they are exchanged with a neighbour who must then try to make a drawing based on the description. When the drawings are complete, they may be compared with the originals and the differences discussed.

23 What's the difference?

Language, topic, type of communication Describing pictures of objects and people, asking questions, making comparisons.

Skills Listening and speaking

Degree of control Free

Level Intermediate/advanced

Time 5–15 minutes

Preparation Each pair of learners will need two pictures which are *very* similar: there should be a few describable differences. (For advanced learners you may decide to have many small differences.)

Procedure Pair work

Divide the class into pairs. (If you have not got enough pictures for everyone, then some pairs can play another pair work game.) Each player gets one picture and does *not* see his partner's picture. Both players may describe their own picture and/or ask questions of the other. The aim is for the players to find the differences between the two pictures.
Finally the two pictures are compared and discussed further.

Variation Copy, or trace, a drawing (a comic cartoon is often suitable).

Then make another copy, but deliberately introduce 7 or 8 differences. You can do this by omitting parts of the original, by making additions, or by making small changes. The two drawings can be presented on flashcards, OHP transparencies, or on photocopied sheets.
The drawings opposite show how this can be done simply.

The learners study the pictures. As soon as someone sees a difference, he describes it to the class, e.g.

In the second picture,

the big monkey's thumb is longer.
the mountain is higher.
the wheel on the lorry is smaller.
the little monkey's ears are bigger.
the man hasn't got a hat on.
there is no headlight on the lorry.
the big monkey is holding a banana.

More advanced learners could be asked to write down all the differences they can find before the oral discussion.
Learners can play this game in pairs making their own drawings.

24 Drawing blind

Language, topic, type of communication	Giving instructions, referring to objects, positions, etc., criticising, encouraging, e.g. *Draw a tree on the right . . . Make it bigger . . . That's right . . .*
Skills	Listening and speaking
Degree of control	Free
Level	Intermediate/advanced
Time	5–10 minutes
Preparation	Prepare a large drawing on paper or OHP transparency. The drawing should be of one or two quite simple and clearly defined objects. See example on p. 46.
Procedure	Class work

A volunteer is blindfolded and, without ever seeing your picture, tries to draw it on the board following instructions called from the class.

25 Are you a good detective?

Language, topic, type of communication	Comparing a written description of a picture with the picture itself, identifying and discussing discrepancies, and composing an accurate description.
Skills	Listening, speaking, reading and writing
Degree of control	Guided
Level	Intermediate/advanced
Time	20–40 minutes
Preparation	Take an interesting photograph from a newspaper or magazine, then write an account of the event shown in the photograph which, in several respects, is at variance with the evidence of the photograph.
Procedure	Class work
	The learners can discuss with you the contradictions between the photograph and the written account before going on to write an account which does not contradict the photograph.
Variation	If you are trying to introduce a class to writing narrative descriptions based on a series of pictures, you will find this game useful. Write a description of the pictures, using the sort of language you would like the learners to use, but making a number of factual errors.
	The learners compare the pictures and your text, reading the text aloud until they see a mistake. They then correct the sentence containing the mistake orally. When all the mistakes have been corrected in this way, the learners can write a corrected narrative.

26 Super sleuth

Language, topic, type of communication	Identifying and discussing the discrepancies between two texts, with use of the past simple.
Skills	Listening, speaking and reading
Degree of control	Guided

47

Level	Intermediate/advanced
Time	20–30 minutes
Preparation	In this game, the learners study similar texts to spot the differences between them. With advanced learners, this can often be done simply by taking articles on the same topic from two different newspapers. Alternatively, the teacher can compose one or both of the texts. The texts could be, for example, the statements of two people accused of a crime, but who claim to have been together miles from the scene of the crime. The statements would contain many examples of past tenses.
Procedure	Class work The learners study the two texts and look for differences. In the case of the alibi example: Learner 1: Stan says that they went to the pub at 8 o'clock and Bert says they went there at 8.30. Learner 2: Yes, and Bert says he bought the drinks, and Stan says that he bought them.

27 Would you make a good witness?

Language, topic, type of communication	Describing people's appearance and actions, using the past continuous (e.g. *He was standing at a bus stop . . .*). In Variation 1, the vocabulary for naming and describing clothing is used. In Variation 2, the past simple is also used (e.g. *He came into the room*).
Skills	Listening and speaking
Degree of control	Free
Level	Intermediate/advanced
Time	10–15 minutes
Preparation	You need a picture of a busy street scene. Sources for such a picture include magazines, tourist publicity, road safety publicity and tourist slides. Ideally, the picture should be big enough to be seen from the back of the class but this is not essential.

Picture games

Procedure Class work

Before showing the picture, ask if any of the learners have witnessed an accident or crime in the street. Discuss with the class the difficulties of being a witness. Then tell them that you are going to show them a picture of a street for a few seconds and that they must try to remember as much of it as they can.

If the picture is big, show it from the front of the class. If it is small, walk slowly about the class, letting the learners look at it as you pass.

Hide the picture and ask the learners to tell you what they saw. You may have to prompt the learners or cross-check their answers, e.g.

Teacher: What did you see in the picture? What can you
            remember?
Learner 1: A man . . .
Teacher: Yes. What was he doing?
Learner 1: He was standing at a bus stop.
Teacher: Was anyone else standing at the bus stop?
Learner 2: Yes, a boy.
Teacher: Can you tell me what he was wearing?
Learner 2: He was wearing a T-shirt and jeans.
Teacher: *Was* he wearing a T-shirt?
Learner 3: No, I think it was a jersey.

Finally, show the picture to the class again.

Warning In case the learners find difficulty in talking about the picture, have a number of questions ready.

Variation 1 To give the learners practice in describing articles of clothing, make a collection of hats, scarves, glasses, coats, etc. Ask one learner to dress up in some of these clothes *outside* the classroom. He or she should then come into the classroom for a few seconds, before going out again. The class must try to describe his or her appearance.

Variation 2 To give practice in the description of clothing and objects and in the use of the past simple and the past continuous, you might like to arrange for a smash-and-grab raid in the classroom!

Before the lesson starts, explain your plan to two learners. They should dress up in strange clothes, enter the classroom, seize a variety of objects, putting some into a bag, others into their pockets and carrying the remainder. They should then leave the classroom. The whole 'crime' should not take more than a few seconds.

49

The two 'criminals' should make sure that everyone can see what they are doing so, for example, they should not turn their backs on the class.
Ask the class to describe the 'criminals'' appearance, what they did and which objects they took.

28 Arrange the pictures

Language, topic, type of communication Describing pictures of objects and people (e.g. *He's holding a pipe*), giving instructions concerning position and sequence, asking questions, encouraging, etc.

Skills Listening and speaking

Degree of control Free

Level Intermediate/advanced

Time 5–15 minutes

Preparation You need two sets of the same pictures. One set should be in a fixed order but the other should not be. If you can find two copies of the same magazine, holiday brochure or comic, one page of pictures can be kept complete and the other cut up.

Procedure Pair work

Give the complete page of pictures to one player and the separate pictures to the other. *The second player must not see the complete version.* The first player then describes the pictures, beginning with the first one, and tells the second player the order to arrange them in. The second player may ask questions, e.g.
Learner 1: There's a man in the first picture. He's holding a pipe but he's not smoking it.
Learner 2: (Picks up the wrong one)
Learner 1: No, I said he *isn't* smoking his pipe.
Learner 2: Oh, sorry. Is it this one with the green curtains?
Learner 1: Yes. Good. Now the second one . . .

The game may, of course, be followed by a short discussion of what happened in the pictures.

29 Who are you?

Language, topic, Questions and answers to establish people's appearance, interests
type of and other details.
communication

Skills Listening, speaking, reading and writing

Degree of control Free

Level Intermediate/advanced

Time 60–80 minutes

Preparation Each learner should have a piece of paper or card about
20cm × 30cm.

Procedure Individual work, leading to class work and pair work

This game or activity is divided into three stages:
1 *Each learner makes a 'biographical card' of a well-known person*
The illustration and writing should be on one side only. The
following information might be included: appearance
(including a photograph or drawing), verbal description, age,
family, job (including a few details), other interests, hobbies,
etc.
2 *All these biographical cards are displayed*
All the learners study the cards on display and write down the
names. They must try to remember the information.
3 *Learners*
Give each learner one of the biographical cards, not necessarily
the one he or she made. Then, working in pairs, the learners
question each other to find out who the other is. The only rule
is that the name should not be asked for. Each learner is then
allowed one guess at the name on the other learner's
biographical card.

30   Picture out of focus

Language, topic, Describing a picture, using language items indicating uncertainty,
type of e.g. *It might be . . . It could be . . .*
communication

Skills Listening and speaking

Degree of control Free

Level Intermediate/advanced

Time 10–15 minutes

Preparation A slide projector and a slide. An OHP and transparency of a
picture would also work but would not provide the same subtlety
of colour.

Procedure Class work

Put the slide into the projector and turn the lens out of focus *before*
you switch on.
Teacher: What can you see?
Learner: Nothing.
Teacher: Nothing?
Learner: Some colours.

Ask the learners to describe what they see and to speculate about
what the colours and indistinct shapes might be.
Bring the slide into focus, stopping perhaps three or four times to
allow people to put forward new conjectures, e.g.
Learner 1: I think those are people on the left and that square
thing above them might be a window.
Learner 2: It *could* be a picture.

Finally, bring the slide into sharp focus.

Sound games

31 Voices and objects

Language, topic, type of communication Naming people and objects in response to a question, *Who am I?* or *What's this?*

Skills Listening and speaking

Degree of control Guided

Level Beginners

Time 5–10 minutes

Preparation You need a blindfold.

Procedure Class work

Blindfold a learner. Ask another learner to come forward and stand quietly next to the first and say something to him, e.g.
Learner 2: Who am I?
Learner 1: Michael?
Learner 2: No, listen.
            Quick, quick,
            The cat's been sick.
            Where? Where?
            Under the chair.
Learner 1: David!
Learner 2: Yes.
Learner 3: What's this?
            (drops object on to desk)
Learner 1: A key.
Learner 3: No, it isn't.
            (drops object again)
Learner 1: A coin.
Learner 3: Yes.

32 Actions by one person

Language, topic, type of communication	Narrating a sequence of events, using the present continuous (e.g. *He's opening some drawers*) and past simple (e.g. *He opened some drawers*).
Skills	Listening and speaking
Degree of control	Guided
Level	Beginners
Time	10–15 minutes
Preparation	Write down a sequence of actions on a piece of paper (see example below).
Procedure	Class work

So often the present continous is practised in the classroom by reference to actions which are seen. In this game the learners close their eyes, listen and try to interpret what they hear.

Ask everyone to close their eyes and put their heads on their arms to reduce the chance of them sneaking a look!

Give a written sequence of actions to one learner to perform, e.g.

Walk quietly across the room to the teacher's desk.
Open and close all the drawers quietly.
Walk quietly to the cupboard.
Open the doors and then close them.
Walk quietly across the room.
Open the classroom door. Go out and close the door.

Ask the learner to do the sequence of actions twice. During the first sequence the class listen and say nothing. During the second sequence you can ask questions, e.g.

Teacher: What is he doing?
Class: He's walking.
Teacher: Is he walking quietly?
Class: Yes.
Teacher: Now, what is he doing?
Class: He's opening some drawers.

For the past simple, ask the class to describe the sequence of actions once they have been performed. If there are mistakes perform the sequence again. Finally let everyone *see* the actions and confirm each description by using the present continuous.

33 Listening to sounds

Language, topic, type of communication — Naming and describing sounds, using the pattern *I can hear . . .* and the present continuous; also uncertainty indicated by *I think I can hear . . .* or *probably.*

Skills — Listening and speaking

Degree of control — Guided

Level — Beginners/intermediate

Time — 5–10 minutes

Preparation — None

Procedure — Class work

Ask everyone to close their eyes, perhaps even to rest their heads on their arms. Ask the learners to listen carefully to every sound they can hear and to try to identify the sounds. They will be listening for all the 'natural' noises of the class room, the building, and outside.

You might ask everyone to listen for 2 or 3 minutes and then to write down what they heard, or you could ask some learners to describe the noises as they hear them, e.g.

Learner 1: I can hear some girls.
I can hear some girls playing.
They are laughing and calling to each other. I think they are playing with a ball. Yes, I can hear it (bouncing).

Learner 2: I think I can hear a plane. It's probably coming into the airport.

34 Actions by more than two people

Language, topic, type of communication — Narrating a sequence of actions, using the past continuous (e.g. *Someone was hammering*), the past simple (e.g. *Someone came in*) and the present perfect (e.g. *He's (just) come into the room*).

Skills — Listening and speaking

Degree of control — Guided

Level	Intermediate
Time	10–15 minutes
Preparation	Write down two copies of a sequence of actions to be performed by two people (see Procedure). You will need a hammer and a piece of wood.
Procedure	Class work

Ask everyone to close their eyes and put their heads on their arms. Select two learners, and give them each a copy of the sequence of actions so that they know what to do, e.g.

A: At teacher's desk: hammers a nail into wood.
B: Opens door of room and says, 'Hi!'
A: Continues to hammer and says 'Hi!' followed immediately by 'Ouch!'
A: Drops hammer.
B: Quickly walks to A and pulls chair across for A to sit on.
A: Groans. Sits on chair, groans again.

Before the class open their eyes, A and B should return to their places.
Teacher: What happened?
Learner 1: Someone was hammering.
Learner 2: Then someone came in.
Learner 2: Then someone said, 'Ouch!'
Teacher: Why did he say, 'Ouch!'?
Learner 3: Because he hit himself with the hammer.
Teacher: Why did the person hit himself.
Learner 4: Probably because he looked up when he said, 'Hi!'

If there is some confusion over the sequence of events tell the class to close their eyes again and ask two learners to perform again. If the sequence was correctly reported ask everyone to watch the sequence again. Comment on it as it happens and then ask for a summary, e.g.

'John was hammering on the desk when Helen came into the room. Helen said "Hi!" and John looked up. When he looked up he hit his finger. Helen came across the room and got a chair. John sat down and groaned.'

If this is followed by some similar sequence the language points will be well practised. The learners, in pairs or groups could be asked to present their own sequences. (See also, 'Using the tape recorder', Game 35, example 3.)

56

Sound games

Warning As this game provides a very realistic situation for the use of a variety of these forms it is essential for you to use the tenses correctly. Particular attention should be given to the present perfect which in this kind of situation is only for reference to acts which have just been completed, e.g. 'He's (just) come into the room'.

35 Using the tape recorder

Language, topic, type of communication Identifying and describing sounds, and narrating sequences of events, using various verb forms: present continuous (*The woman is singing*); present perfect (*He has opened the door*); past simple (*The dog barked*); future (*He's going to open a drawer*); expressing uncertainty (*I'm not sure . . . It could be . . .*)

Skills Listening and speaking

Degree of control Guided

Level Intermediate and advanced

Time 20–30 minutes

Preparation Record, or ask your learners to record, the various sounds listed below under Procedure.
Some excellent published material of this type is available: *Sounds Interesting*, by Alan Maley and Alan Duff, CUP, 1975 (Teacher's Book, and tape or cassette); and *Sounds Intriguing*, by Alan Maley and Alan Duff, CUP, 1979 (Teacher's Book and cassette).

Procedure Class work or group work

Below are three examples of the use of taped sounds.

Example 1
Door opening/closing – cigarette being lit – car being started and driven away – telephone ringing and being answered – watch and clock ticking – floor being brushed – cupboard being locked – dog barking – someone sneezing.

Questions include: (just before playing the sound) What is this?; (still playing) Is it a . . .?; (after playing) Was it a . . .? What was that? What was he doing? What was happening?

Example 2
For the present perfect we need an event (more than a minor

57

action) which has *just* been completed.

i)   Washing up – pots put to dry – water poured away.
ii) Alarm clock – groan of waking person – 'Oh dear!'
iii) Typing-paper removed – pen signature made.
iv) Door opens – class comes in – they settle down.

Questions include: What has (just) happened?

Example 3 (sounds in sequence)
For the past simple a narrative episode is ideal. A sound story like
the one described below may also involve the use of various tense
forms.
While the tape is playing: present continuous (*The woman is
singing*) and present simple (*She has some keys*); when you have
stopped the tape: present perfect (*He has opened the door*) and past
simple + while + past continuous (*The dog barked while she was
phoning the police*); when you play the tape again and stop it before
the action: future with going to (*He's going to open a drawer and
take some money*).

Radio music – radio switched off – door opened – bath water run
– singing of woman – splashes in bath (fades) – wind – car stops –
door opens and closes – footsteps up drive – rattle of keys – door
opens – little dog barks, then is kicked and howls – footsteps in
hall (tiptoeing) – door opened – drawer opened – money clinking
– footsteps – dog snarls – door opened – scream of woman – splash
of bath water – running of feet – opening and closing of door –
splash of water – wet feet – telephone being dialled (3 numbers) –
dog barks again – dog kicked – howls again.

Warning   Material of this kind will be enjoyable and game-like as long as
the emphasis is placed on the mystery of sound and the fun of
interpreting it. Such material will become ordinary if the teacher
tries to 'squeeze' too many language teaching points out of it.

Word games

36 The odd man out

Language, topic, type of communication	Giving reasons, using *because*, answering questions, agreeing and disagreeing. The game is ideal for revising lexical sets, e.g. words for colours, family relations, animals, household utensils.
Skills	Listening, speaking, reading and writing
Degree of control	Guided
Level	Intermediate, Variation advanced
Time	10 minutes
Preparation	Prepare 10–15 groups of words, each of which contains an 'odd man out', e.g.

i)   horse, cow, mouse, *knife*, fish
ii) David, Michael, Andrew, *Alison*, Adrian
iii) *plate*, bean, soup, sandwich, apple
iv) *bicycle*, bus, car, motorcycle, lorry
v) green, *big*, orange, brown, red
vi) brother, father, *sister*, uncle, grandfather
vii) June, January, March, *Spring*, May
viii) Austin, *Volvo*, Morris, Jaguar
ix) Shakespeare, Milton, J. B. Priestley, *Laurence Olivier*
x)   Paris, Ottawa, *New York*, London

The words used should, of course, reflect the interests of the learners and could be of a specialist nature.
They can be presented on a chalk board, an OHP, or on sheets of paper.

Procedure	Class work

The learners write down the word from the first group which they think is the 'odd man out'. Individuals are then asked to say which is the 'odd man out' and to say why.
The other players should be asked if they agree; if they disagree,

to say why. The teacher should not say which answer he thinks is correct until this discussion is finished – partly because this would inhibit discussion and partly because there may be no *one* correct answer, and the learners should be encouraged to find as many possible answers as they can. Each of the groups of words can be discussed in turn in this way.

If any learner experiences difficulty here, the teacher can help by asking leading questions, for example, for x) above:

Teacher: What is the capital of France/Canada/the U.S.A./ England?

Variation This game is for advanced learners and mainly for use in group work or pair work.

Words should be selected which have no *obvious* connection. The words could be photocopied for each group or could be on the board or OHP, e.g. knife, saucepan, box, ruler, cabbage, bottle, typewriter, hammer, book.

The aim of the game is to find different ways of classifying *four* of the words in each group. It is essential that the player can argue the case for his proposed classification, however eccentric it may be.

Common ways of classifying may refer to the material the objects are made of, their usage, their size, cost or shape. Less common classifications might be origin (for example, cabbage is not found in West Africa but the other objects are); or naturalness (cabbage is grown and not manufactured like the others); or more unexpected classifications (for example, typewriter has ten letters and all the others have eight letters or less).

Warning The game will work only if the learners have sufficient command of the language to be able to name such categories as *size, quantity, quality, speed* and *texture* – that is to say, the categories which unite the companion words in each game. You may have to teach the learners the words for these categories, concentrating on a few each time you play 'Odd man out', and directing the learners to confine themselves to these when they devise their own examples.

37 Connections

Language, topic, type of communication	Asking for and giving reasons, using *Why . . .?* and *Because . . .*
Skills	Listening and speaking
Degree of control	Guided
Level	Intermediate/advanced
Time	5–10 minutes
Preparation	None
Procedure	Class, group or pair work

Each learner in turn says a word he associates with the word given by the learner before him. This should be done as a fast game. Sometimes you or another learner may interrupt and ask why a word was chosen, e.g.

Learner 1 : Water.
Learner 2 : Tap.
Learner 3 : Shoulder.
Teacher: Why did you say shoulder?
Learner 3 : Because I thought of the sentence, 'A tap on the shoulder!'
Learner 4 : Coat.
Learner 5 : Joseph.
Teacher: Why did you say Joseph?
Learner 5 : Because Joseph had a famous coat.
Learner 6 : Egypt.

38 Definitions

Language, topic, type of communication	Asking for and giving definitions of words. The question word *What . . .?* is used, also *How . . .? Where . . .?* etc.
Skills	Listening and speaking
Degree of control	Guided

Word games

Level	Advanced
Time	10–15 minutes
Preparation	Choose a few words for the learners to define. Here are some examples: wall, typewriter, window, drum, garage, pen, ice-cream, cup of tea, penny, slice of bread.
Procedure	Class work, leading to pair work

Giving definitions of words may appear to be a traditional language learning activity! However, the approach below transforms this rather dull business into an exciting challenge! The idea is to continually challenge the player to define nearly every word he says, so that he is compelled to define the words that he is using to define the words that he is using . . . to define the word you originally gave him to define. Other learners should, of course, be asked to join in, by asking them to define words, e.g.

Teacher: What does 'wall' mean?
Learner 1: A wall is a vertical division, often made out of stone, bricks or concrete.
Learner 2: What is concrete?
Learner 1: Concrete is a material made out of sand, cement and small stones.
Learner 3: What is cement?
Learner 1: Cement is made out of limestone.
(Most questions will begin with *What . . . ?* However, you may ask *How . . . ?* and *Where . . . ?* etc.)
Learner 4: How is limestone made into cement?
Learner 1: Er . . . I don't know!

You should limit each game by allowing no more than 6 requests for definitions or by an admission of inability to define a word.

Warning	Too strict a control over the grammatical form of the definitions will curtail goodwill and willingness to 'have a go'. Encourage a light-hearted, inventive and occasionally fanciful attitude!

62

Story games

39 Silly stories

Language, topic,
type of
communication

Making up stories, using the past tense and reported speech.

Skills Listening and speaking

Degree of control Free

Level Intermediate/advanced

Time 5–10 minutes

Preparation None, unless you would like to think of some beginnings for stories (see below).

Procedure Class work

Begin the story with the first half of a sentence. Then ask the class to think of a continuation, e.g.
Teacher: I saw a horse sitting . . .
Learner 1: . . . in the kitchen.
Teacher: It was eating . . .
Learner 2: . . . a piece of cake.
Learner 3: And drinking a cup of tea.
Teacher: I said . . .
Learner 4: 'Don't you have milk in your tea?'

40   Fantasy stories

Language, topic, type of communication	Making up stories, using all the language at the learner's command, particularly past tense verb forms.
Skills	Listening, speaking, reading and writing
Degree of control	Free
Level	Intermediate/advanced
Time	30 minutes
Preparation	Each pair or group will need 15–20 pictures cut from magazines. *Any* pictures will do, but they should show a variety of places and objects and include several people.
Procedure	Group or pair work, leading to class work

The object of the game is to invent a complete fantasy based on the pictures received. It should *not* be realistic about someone losing their purse or having a party, for example. The pair or group should invent the story through discussion.
Once the story is ready, it should be written down and/or recorded on tape.
The stories should then be told to the whole class.
The pictures and the written version of the stories could be displayed on the wall.

Variation 1   Instead of giving each pair or group a selection of pictures, put 15–20 pictures on the walls of the class room.
Then ask the pairs or groups to invent a story, making use of the pictures *in any order.*
When everyone has finished, the stories can be written down and told.
The advantage of this variation is that each group will be more interested in what the others have written, because the same pictures have been used.

Variation 2   Instead of using only pictures, prepare a kit containing 6–10 assorted objects and pictures, e.g. a piece of string, a key, a toy car, a picture of an expensive house, a picture of a bank, a whistle, an empty purse or wallet.
Each group works independently to prepare a short play to

'reconstruct a crime', and must refer to all the objects and pictures. Each play is then presented to the class.

Variation 3 Each learner in a group is given a picture or an object. The learners then take turns to tell a story. They must continue the story as told by their neighbour and must refer to the picture or object at some point in their continuation of the story.

41 Alibis

Language, topic, Asking questions, giving answers, and narrating past events.
type of Many question forms are practised: *Where . . .? Who . . .? Why*
communication *. . .? Did . . .?* etc.

Skills Listening and speaking

Degree of control Free

Level Intermediate/advanced

Time 30 minutes for the learners to prepare an alibi, and 10–15 minutes to play.

Preparation None

Procedure Pair work, leading to class work

Each pair imagine that they have to create an alibi for a given evening. They work together to produce a story which accounts for every minute between 7 pm and 10 pm on that evening. They then try to memorise the story. This preparation can take place outside the class room, if wished.

When the alibi has been prepared, one of the two who have prepared it waits outside while the other faces the rest of the class. The class question him or her at length to find out the details of the alibi. Then his or her partner comes in and is subjected to a similar interrogation. The class try to find inconsistencies in the stories and look for contradictions. If they find any, the alibi is broken and the class win. If not, the two who made up the alibi win.

Many question forms will be used, e.g.

Learners: Where were you at 7.15?
Who else was there?
What time did you leave?

What did you do next?
Why did you go there?
Whose idea was it to go there?
How much did it cost?
Who paid?
Did you get any change?
When did you leave?
How did you get home?

42 Confabulation, or the key sentence

Language, topic,   Making up a story or play around a given sentence.
type of
communication

Skills   Listening, speaking and writing

Degree of control   Free

Level   Advanced

Time   30–40 minutes

Preparation   None

Procedure   Group or pair work, leading to class work

Each group or pair is given an unlikely sentence which is kept a
secret from the others, e.g.
I always eat trout for breakfast.
I opened the door and saw an elephant.
So I replied, 'Never on a Sunday'.
Each group prepares a story or a play which includes the sentence
exactly as it has been given, as naturally as possible. The group
tells the story or acts out the play for the others, who have to try
to spot the given sentence.

Party games

43   Kaboom

Language, topic,   Describing actions, both in the past (*I picked up the coin*) and in the
type of   future (*I'm going to pick up the coin*). The negative is used in both (*I*
communication   *didn't pick up . . .* and *I'm not going to pick up . . .*).

Skills   Listening and speaking

Degree of control   Teacher-controlled

Level   Beginners
This trick has obvious appeal to young learners. However, older
people might like to learn it in order to try it out on their children
or younger brothers or sisters.

Time   2–3 minutes to demonstrate the trick.
20 minutes for all learners to learn the trick in pair work.

Preparation   You need a small, flat object, for example, a coin or a small piece
of paper. You also need a bigger object to cover the smaller one,
for example, a book or a plate.

Procedure   Class work leading to pair work

Hold up the small object so that all the class can identify it. Put it
on the table. Hold up the larger object also for identification. Put
the larger object on top of the smaller object. Then say:
I'm going to pick up the (coin).
But I'm not going to pick up the (book).
Kaboom!
(Invite a learner to come to the desk and to look underneath the
big object. As the learner does so, pick up the small object.) Then
say:
I picked up the (coin).
But I didn't pick up the (book).
You did!

Ask the learners if they would like to learn the trick to try out on
others.
Get a number of them to try the trick out in front of the class.
When you are confident that everyone has learned the words and
actions, ask them to practise it in pairs.
It helps the transition to pair work if you write the sentences on
the board as above.

Warning Choose someone to look underneath the (book) who is not too
much of a sceptic! He might refuse. Say to him or her
encouragingly, 'Have a look!'

44 The matchbox

Language, topic,
type of
communication Asking questions and making statements, with use of *some* and *any*.

Skills Listening and speaking

Degree of control Teacher-controlled

Level Beginners

Time 3–5 minutes to do the trick.
20 minutes for all learners to learn the trick.

Preparation You need two matchboxes. One of them should be half full of
matches and placed inside your right sleeve. You may have to
fasten it to your forearm with a rubber band. The other box, also
half full of matches, should be on the desk in front of you.
For pair work you will need the same materials for each pair. If
this proves difficult, then you will only be able to let a few learners
try the trick.

Procedure Class work leading to pair work

Hold up the box on the table and shake it.
Teacher: Are there any matches in the box?
Class: Yes.
Teacher: (Pointing at one learner) Do you think there are any
          matches in the box?
Learner: Yes.
Teacher: (Open the box and take the matches out.) Are there any

matches in the box now?

Class: No!

Teacher: (Shake the closed box with your left hand.) Are there any matches in it now?

Class: No!

Teacher: (Shake the box with your right hand. There will seem to be matches in it because the ones inside your sleeve will be rattling!) Are there any matches in it?

Class: No!... Yes!

Teacher: (Open the box in your hand.) Are there any matches in it?

Class: No (there aren't).

Teacher: (Now shake it first with your left then with your right hand. Ask the question each time. Finally the learners will realise that you have a matchbox up your sleeve. Reveal it and remove it.) Are there any matches in *this* box?

Class: Yes!

Teacher: (Open the box and show the matches.) Yes, there are some matches in it!

(Show the empty box.) There aren't any matches in this box. But there are some in this one.

Show one or two learners how to do the trick and what to say. Then organise the activity as pair work. It would be helpful if you put the following sentences on the board.

Are there any ... in this box?
Yes, there are.
No, there aren't.
There aren't any ... but there are some ...

45   Fortune teller

Language, topic, type of communication	Asking questions with *Who ...?* and *What ...?* Reading prepared sentences containing reference to the future with *will*.
Skills	Listening, speaking, reading and writing
Degree of control	Guided
Level	Beginners

Party games

Time   30–40 minutes

Preparation   This device, folded in paper, is known to children in many
countries. If you are not sure how it is made, ask some children
aged 9 or 10.
Have one of these ready before the class begins. Names and
numbers are usually written on the outside surfaces. On the inside
eight sentences are written, referring to the future.

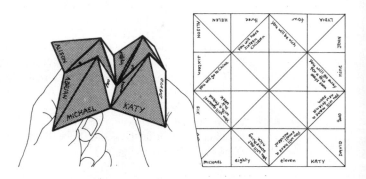

Procedure   Class work leading to pair work

Show the class your fortune teller and tell one or two fortunes.
The usual exchange between English children is as follows:
A: Who do you love? (referring to one of the names on the
fortune teller).
B: Michael.
A: M-I-C-H-A-E-L (opens and shuts the device as he says the
letters). What number do you want?
B: 8.
A: 1, 2, 3, 4, 5, 6, 7, 8 (opens and shuts the device as he says the
numbers). What number do you want now?
B: 3.
A: (Opens the flap with the number 3 written on it and reads out
the fortune written beneath.) You will go to China!

On the assumption that at least some people in the class will know
how to make the device, ask everyone to prepare eight
appropriate original sentences referring to the future, e.g.
You will go to China.
You will have 16 children.
Organise the making of the devices so that each learner has one
and can write on one side the eight sentences referring to the
future and, on the other, names and numbers.

46 Climbing through a postcard

Language, topic, Talking about the action of climbing through a postcard, using
type of *going to* (*I'm going to climb through it*), the present continuous (*I'm*
communication *climbing through it*), and the present perfect (*I've climbed through it*).

Skills Listening and speaking

Degree of control Teacher-controlled

Level Beginners/intermediate

Time 2–3 minutes to demonstrate the trick.
20 minutes for all learners to prepare their card and climb through
it.

Preparation You need one postcard or a plain piece of card of postcard size or
larger, and a pair of scissors. Have enough card or paper for each
learner.

Procedure Class work leading to pair work

Ask if anyone can climb through the piece of card. Ask if *they*
think *you* can. Now cut the card as shown in the diagram below.

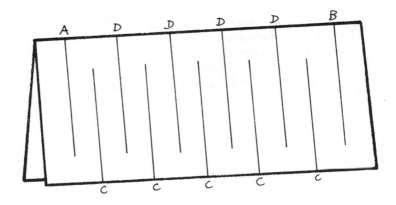

1 Fold it in half lengthways.
2 Make two cuts A, B.
3 Cut along fold from A to B.
4 Now do alternate cuts C, D, C, D, etc.
As you prepare the card say:
Teacher: I'm going to cut the card.
I'm cutting the card.
I've cut the card.

Now shake out the zigzag circle of card and climb through it, not forgetting to say:
Teacher: I'm going to climb through it.
I'm climbing through it.
I've climbed through it.

If you *don't* want to climb through it, ask a learner to go through it for you. You can then introduce, 'He's going to . . .' etc.
Organise pair work in the usual way, making sure that everyone knows how to cut the card.
Write the six sentences on the board.
Suggest that the trick is well practised so that it can be demonstrated to friends or other classes without fault. And this means frequent repetition of the language!

47 The piece of string

Language, topic, type of communication	Talking about a trick, using *going to* (*I'm going to cut* . . .), the present continuous (*I'm cutting* . . .), and the present perfect (*I've mended it*).
Skills	Listening, speaking and reading
Degree of control	Teacher-controlled
Level	Beginners/intermediate
Time	2–3 minutes to demonstrate the trick. 20 minutes for all learners to learn the trick in pair work.
Preparation	You need a piece of string about 20cm long and another piece *of the same type* about 8cm long. You also need a pair of scissors. Each pair of learners will also have to be equipped in the same way if they are to practise the trick.
Procedure	Class work leading to pair work

Before the class begins, fold the smaller piece of string in half and keep it in your hand. (The hand you do *not* use for scissors!) At the beginning of the trick take up the longer piece of string, fold it in half and place it next to the other.

Then, with the point of your scissors raise the bend of the *shorter* piece of string and slowly cut it.

Then scramble *all* the string into your hand and say you are mending it.

Then take one end of the long piece of string and pull it sharply, claiming that it has been mended. As your arm surges upwards, drawing people's attention in that direction, drop the two little pieces of cut string on the floor.

Teacher: I'm going to cut this piece of string. (Hold the string up.)
I'm cutting it. (Cut the short piece of string.)
I've cut it. (Indicate the cut ends.)
Now . . .
I'm going to mend it. (Put all string in hand.)
I'm mending it. (Squeeze it and look magical.)
I've mended it. (Pull out long piece of string, drop short piece.)

Of course, someone will eventually notice the pieces of string on the floor. Then you can offer to teach the trick to them.

For pair work it would be advisable to demonstrate the trick with one or two learners to ensure that the sequence of events is understood.

Write the six sentences on the board.

After some practice, you might remove the sentences from the board.

48 Consequences

Language, topic, type of communication Making up sentences, using the past tense according to a given pattern; asking questions and giving answers about the sentences.

Skills Listening, speaking, reading and writing

Degree of control Guided

Level Intermediate

Time 10 minutes

Party games

Preparation	A piece of paper for each learner
Procedure	Group work leading to class work

Demonstrate the idea. Fold a piece of paper into half, quarters and eighths; all the folds should be parallel. Then, guided by these folds, refold the paper into a concertina. As each person writes, he should only look at his fold.

Learner 1: ... (a man's name)
    met
Learner 2: ... (a woman's name)
    at/in
Learner 3: ... (a place)
Learner 4: He said ...
Learner 5: She said ...
Learner 6: And so they ...

Winston Churchill
met
Doris Day
in
the Tower of London
He said, Do you like dancing?
She said, You're too fat.
And so they drank tea.

When the last person has written on the last fold ask him to read it all out.
Other versions in this 'story' might be as follows:

Learner 1: If ...	If ...
met	had met
Learner 2: ...	...
in	at
Learner 3: ...	...
Learner 4: He would say ...	He would have said ...
Learner 5: She would answer ...	She would have answered ...
Learner 6: And so they would ...	And so they would have ...

There could be some discussion of the results, but discussion should be in the spirit of the game and not become mere mechanical transformation of tenses, e.g.
Who met A? Who did B meet? Where did they meet? What did he/she say? What happened? What would he/she really have said? What would you say if you met A in a bookshop?

Variation	In many countries it is customary, on New Year's Day, to promise improved behaviour for the following year. The idea of the 'New Year's Resolution' provides a basis for a variation of the 'Consequences' game.
Procedure	Group work leading to class work

Each group or row of players has a sheet of paper. The first player writes: I, (name), *promise to* ...

74

Then he folds the paper so that what he has written is hidden and passes the paper to the next player. This player writes a New Year's Resolution, e.g. *stop smoking/work harder*, etc.
He folds the paper again and passes it on. The third player writes: *provided that* (name) *promises to* . . .
He again folds the paper and passes it on to a fourth player who writes a second New Year's Resolution.
The whole message is passed to a fifth player who reads it out to the class.

49 Palmistry

Language, topic, type of communication	Describing people's characters, using the language of amazement, concern, condolence, etc. The future is referred to, using both *will* and *going to*.
Skills	Listening and speaking
Degree of control	Free
Level	Advanced
Time	30–60 minutes
Preparation	Make a big copy of the hand on p. 76 on a large piece of paper or on an OHP transparency.
Procedure	Class work combined with pair or individual work

Ask the learners to trace round their own hands, to draw in the lines and, referring to your big picture of a hand, to interpret the lines and write a description of their own characters. With the class as a whole, debate the accuracy of these descriptions and predictions.
Additionally, you might be able to photocopy various people's hands, and ask the class to interpret them and try to name the owners!

There is not enough space in this book to provide an analysis of the shape and lines of the hand. However, books on this subject are readily available.

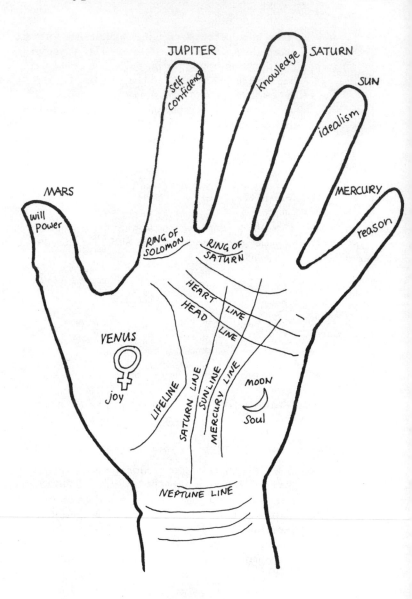

Psychology games

50   Telepathy

Language, topic,   Reading given texts out loud
type of
communication

Skills   Listening and reading

Degree of control   Teacher-controlled

Level   Beginners

Time   10–15 minutes

Preparation   Chalkboard or OHP

Procedure   Class work

Ask if anyone in the class believes in telepathy. (You will probably
do this in your mother tongue.) Say that you intend to carry out
an experiment to test telepathic communication.
Write four short texts on the board.
Ask one learner, who is prepared to be a 'medium', to think of
one of the texts.
Ask the rest of the class, whether they believe in telepathy or not,
to try to concentrate on which they think the 'medium' has
chosen and to write down that particular text.
After two minutes, ask each learner to read out his text, in turn.
(In this activity it is remarkable how everyone *wants* to listen to
everyone else. Everyone wants to be right!)
Ask someone to stand by the chalk board and to place a tick beside
each text as it is referred to.
When all the ticks have been added up, ask the 'medium' to say
which text he or she was thinking of. Decide whether he or she
has managed to transmit their thoughts!

51 Visual perception of length

Language, topic, type of communication	Making statements about length, using comparatives (*longer, shorter*) and superlatives (*longest, shortest*); using possessives (e.g. *John's line*) and names of colours; expressing conjecture (*I think ...*).
Skills	Listening and speaking
Degree of control	Guided
Level	Beginners
Time	2–3 minutes for class work. 20 minutes for pair work.
Preparation	For class work you need a chalk board and a large sheet of paper or the OHP, coloured chalks or pens (4 or 5), and a ruler. For pair work you need paper, coloured pens and rulers.
Procedure	Class work, leading to pair work

Four or five learners take it in turns to draw a line on the board. Each line should be in a different colour, of a different length and be straight. (The lengths should not be too varied.) It helps the game if the lines are crossed.
Challenge the class to judge which is the longest, and which the shortest line, e.g.
Teacher: Which is the longest line, Rachel?
Learner 1: John's line.
Teacher: What do you think, Robin?
Learner 2: I think Mary's line is the longest.

You will find it natural to use the comparative forms as you discuss the opinions put forward.
Teacher: Don't you think the red line is longer than the green line, Robin?

To cause the learners to use the comparative form:
Teacher: I think the blue line is longer than the brown line. What do you think, David?
Learner: I think it's shorter.

After some further discussion you might then ask each learner to write down his judgements, e.g.
Learners: The green line is the shortest line.
The red line is longer than the green line.

78

The brown line is longer than the red line.
The white line is the longest.
Finally, measure the lines and write the measurements next to
them.

Pair work

Each learner draws, with a ruler, a number of coloured lines on a
piece of paper. Below the lines he writes a number of sentences,
some true and some deliberately false, concerning the relative
lengths, e.g.
The red line is longer than the green line.
The brown line is longer than the black line.
The green line is shorter than the brown line.
The pieces of paper are then interchanged and the receiver must
decide, judging by eye, which of the statements are true and
which false.

52   The old woman and the young woman

Language, topic, Identifying physical features in pictures (e.g. *This is the/her nose*,
type of etc.). There is an opportunity for using expressions of
communication astonishment (e.g. *Oh yes!* or *Good Lord!*).

Skills Listening and speaking

Degree of control Guided

Level Beginners

Time 5–10 minutes

Preparation You will need a slide or a large copy of the picture on p. 80.

Procedure Class work

Show the picture without comment for about one minute. Some
of the class will see an *old* woman and some will see a *young*
woman.
Ask the class what they can see in the picture and show some
astonishment that there are quite contradictory opinions about it.
You might ask how many can see the young woman and how
many can see the old woman.
Finally, ask someone to indicate on the picture the person that *they*
can see, e.g.

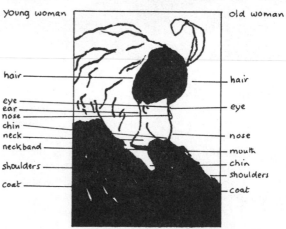

young woman

old woman

hair ———————————————— hair

eye ——
ear ——
nose ——
chin ——
neck ——
neckband ——

shoulders ——

coat ——

eye

nose

mouth
chin
shoulders
coat

Learner: This is the nose.
This is the chin.

53 Blobs

Language, topic, type of communication   Describing, particularly by analogy, e.g. *It looks like a bird . . .*

Skills   Listening and speaking

Degree of control   Guided, except in the Variation, where less control of language is possible or desirable

Level   Beginners/intermediate, except for the Variation, which is aimed at advanced learners

Time   10–15 minutes of playing time. Allow another 10–15 minutes if the pupils are going to make their own blob pictures.

Preparation   The aim in the preparation is to make an abstract collection of shapes and marks. You may do this in any of the following ways:
a) Arrange a number of pieces of torn paper, sand, string, paint, etc. on the screen of the OHP.
b) Splatter, pat and dab some coloured paints or inks on to a large piece of paper.
c) Scribble and smudge pencils and crayons on paper.
d) Place a piece of thin paper on an irregular rough surface and rub a soft black crayon on it.

Procedure   Class work leading to pair work

Show the blob picture to the class. Ask if they can see anything in it. If no ideas are forthcoming you might ask, e.g.
Teacher: Can you see an animal?
or I think this looks like a bird. It's flying. Here are its wings. Here's its head and its beak, etc.
When a learner sees something in the blob pictures, ask him to identify the various parts.

Pair work
Learners can make their own blob pictures using the methods described above. They can then discuss what they see, and write on the picture labelling the different parts of the thing they can see.

Variation   The famous Swiss psychiatrist Rorschach believed that people's interpretations of blob pictures reveal their personalities. He believed that a concern with white spaces shows a negative attitude; concern with bright colour shows an emotional character; concern with various tones shows a trivial and vacillating character; concern with minute detail shows a compulsive nature. These beliefs might be used with advanced learners to stimulate a discussion of people's interpretations and their personality.

54   How quickly can you see?

Language, topic, type of communication   Describing pictures, with special use of the past continuous (e.g. *He was running*).

Skills   Listening and speaking

Degree of control   Guided

Level   All

Time   5–10 minutes

Preparation   You need a collection of pictures no bigger than magazine page size. The pictures may be photographs or drawings and may be on paper, OHP transparency or slide.
If you are concentrating on a particular language teaching point, then you must collect the pictures accordingly (see examples below).

Procedure   Class work leading to pair work

Explain that you are going to test the learners' ability to see at great speed. It is a challenge of their power to react quickly.
Flash a picture at the class, first making sure that everyone has a chance to see it – there should be no heads in the way and the angle should not be too acute for players on each side of the class.

(Picture of a man running)
Teacher: What was he doing?
Learner: (He was) running.

(Picture of 5 sheep)
Teacher: What did you see?
Learner: Some sheep.

Teacher: How many did you see?
Learner: Five.

(Picture of two men)
Teacher: What did you see?
Learner: Two men.
Teacher: What were they doing?
Learner: One was standing and the other was sitting.
Teacher: Which man was standing?
Learner: The one who was wearing a hat.

(Picture of two girls)
Teacher: What did you see?
Learner: Two girls.
Teacher: Which one was the taller?
Learner: The one in the blue hat.

(Picture of a packet of cigarettes)
Teacher: What did you see?
Learner: A packet of cigarettes.
Teacher: Was it a new one or had it been opened?
Learner: It had been opened.

55 Faces and character

Language, topic, type of communication — Describing people, speculating about age, character, etc. (e.g. *He might be . . .*).

Skills — Listening and speaking

Degree of control — Free

Level — Intermediate/advanced

Time — 5 minutes for a discussion of each photograph you choose to show.

Preparation — For class work you will need a minimum of three or four photographs of people you know or know about. The pictures should be large enough for class use. (Projected slides would be ideal.)
For pair work, the pupils must be equipped in a similar way. They could be asked to bring pictures from home of their family, friends or anyone else who will be unknown to other learners in the class.

Procedure   Class work leading to pair work

First discuss with the class how reliable people's appearance is as a guide to their age, interests, background, character, etc. You might tell them that it was commonly believed in the last century that one could recognise a criminal by the shape of his ears! Then say that you will show a picture of someone you know well and that you will ask the class to suggest as much as they can to you about the person. Finally confirm, qualify or reject these speculations by describing the person yourself.

56   Visual imagery

Language, topic,   Using any appropriate language to describe mental pictures.
type of
communication

Skills   Speaking and/or writing

Degree of control   Free

Level   Advanced

Time   5–10 minutes

Preparation   None

Procedure   Class work

Psychologists of perception have established that the majority of people see pictures in the mind quite apart from their dreams. Most people see these pictures just before going to sleep. However, it is quite possible to see them at other times, when the eyes are closed.
This activity needs considerable understanding between members of the class as it involves personal and, perhaps, private feelings. If you have a suitable class then you might try it.
Here is an example of what might be 'seen'. 'I can see waves crashing on the shore and palm trees bending in the wind. Now I am looking down into some water plants. I can see a nest with pale blue eggs in it.'

Bingo games

57   Number bingo

Language, topic,
type of
communication

Listening to and reading numbers, or, in Variation 1, words, or, in Variation 2, whole sentences. The words and sentences can be selected to practise any area of language that you wish.

Skills

Listening, speaking, reading and writing

Degree of control

Teacher-controlled

Level

Beginners, except for Variation 2, which is suitable for intermediate learners also.

Time

10–20 minutes

Preparation

Paper and pencil for the teacher and each learner.

Procedure

Class work

Decide on a group of numbers you wish to practise, totalling not more than about twenty-five. These may be sequences (e.g. 1–25) or a selection of numbers which present listening problems (e.g. 13 and 30, 19 and 90). Either write them on the board or tell the learners what they are.

Tell the learners to write down any four of the numbers from those you have given them. Call the numbers in random order. The learners must cross out the numbers they have written if they hear them called. The first learner to cross out all four of his or her numbers calls out 'Bingo' and reads out the four numbers to prove the claim.

It is possible to play the game selecting more than four numbers from a group larger than twenty-five. However, this will take more time.

Warning

Make a note of each number as you call it out. This will help you to avoid calling out the numbers more than once.

Variation 1   Instead of listing out twenty-five numbers, as above, choose a group of words you would like the learners to revise, for example, concerning clothing, office equipment, food, etc.
Write these on the board and follow the procedure described above.
Instead of calling out four of the words you may choose to give four definitions of words on the board. This makes the game more of a challenge.

Variation 2   Write or ask the learners to write, about ten short sentences on the board. These might all include prepositions, e.g.
The chemist's shop is on the right of the bank.
The chemist's shop is in front of the bank.
The bank is on the right of the post office, behind the library.
The grocer's shop is behind the library.
The toilets are in the park.
The toilets are in front of the park.
The road goes over the bridge.
The road goes under the bridge.
The sentences may also concern actions, perhaps taken from a picture or pictures, e.g.
The man is drinking tea.
The electrician is repairing the plug.
The woman is typing.
The learners choose any four sentences and illustrate them with quick sketches.
The game is then played as in 'Number Bingo' above.
By using pictures, the learner's attention is focussed on the meaning of the sentences, whereas in Variation 1 the learners merely associate the sound of a word with its written form.

Miscellaneous games

58 Zip

Language, topic, type of communication   Calling out numbers according to a given formula.

Skills   Listening and speaking

Degree of control   Teacher-controlled

Level   Beginners

Time   5–10 minutes

Preparation   None

Procedure   Class or group work

The aim of the game is for the learners to count round the class from 1 to 100 without saying a chosen number or a multiple of it. For example, if you and the class choose 4 they must not say 4, 8, 12, 16, 20, etc. Instead of saying one of these numbers the player, whose turn it is, must say 'Zip!', e.g.

Learner 1: One.
Learner 2: Two.
Learner 3: Three.
Learner 4: Zip!
Learner 5: Five.

59 Bumps under the cloth

Language, topic, type of communication	Asking questions and giving answers, naming objects, expressing doubt, e.g. *I think it's a . . . It could be a . . . I'm not sure . . .*
Skills	Listening and speaking
Degree of control	Guided
Level	Beginners/intermediate, or advanced in the Variation
Time	2–3 minutes to demonstrate the game to the class. Another 10 minutes or more for pair work.
Preparation	Collect about 10 small objects of different shapes and sizes. A piece of cloth, a thin towel, a headscarf, or a large handkerchief will be required. It must be large enough to cover 4 or 5 of the objects.
Procedure	Class work leading to optional pair work

Make sure that the learners know the names of at least the majority of objects which you have collected.
Put 4 or 5 of the objects under the cloth on a table without the class seeing which ones you have chosen.
Ask a learner to feel one of the objects through the cloth and to tell you what he or she thinks it is. If correct, let the learner remove the object. Ask other learners to do the same for the other objects.
The language in this game can be restricted, e.g.
Teacher: What is it?
Learner: It's a . . .
Any of the following language might be used according to your wishes
Teacher: What do you think it is?
Learner: I think it's a . . .
It could be a . . .
I'm not sure . . .
I don't know . . .
I know what it is but I don't know what it's called.
I know what it's called in (Swedish) but I don't know what it's called in English.
If you think that the learners, divided into pairs, can collect a sufficient number of objects, you will find the game easy to arrange for pair work.

Variation Advanced learners might be asked to talk about each feature of the object they are feeling in such a way that the rest of the class can identify it. This will require the use of descriptive terms and the language of speculation, e.g.
Learner 1 : It's hard.
Learner 2 : What's it made of?
Learner 1 : I think it's made of metal.
Learner 3 : What shape is it?
Learner 1 : It's got two round bits. You can put your fingers through them. It's got two long bits which are sharp.
Learner 4 : Is it a pair of scissors?
Learner 1 : Yes, I think so.

60   One idea at a time

Language, topic, type of communication   Describing things using adjectives.
Variation 1 : adverbs (e.g. *noisily*) and imperatives (e.g. *open, close*);
Variation 2 : names of jobs and questions; Variation 3 : present continuous (e.g. *You're carrying something*); Variation 4 : present perfect (e.g. *Have you hurt . . .?*)

Skills   Listening and speaking

Degree of control   Guided

Level   Beginners/intermediate

Time   10–15 minutes

Preparation   None

Procedure   Class work

One learner mimes an adjective and the others try to guess what he is miming, e.g.
Learner 1 : Are you tired?
Mimer :   (Shakes head)
Learner 2 : Are you lazy?
Mimer :   (Shakes head)
Learner 3 : Are you bored?
Mimer :   (Nods head)
You should then encourage the other learners to find the reason for his boredom, e.g.
Learner 4 : Are you bored because you have nothing to do?

Other examples: miserable, busy, thirsty, frightened, surprised, angry.

Variation 1   *Adverbs and imperatives*
One learner chooses an adverb which will be easy to demonstrate, whatever action he is asked to do. The class then ask him to perform various actions and try to guess the adverb he has chosen. For example, he may have chosen 'angrily'.
Class: Open and close the door.
Mimer: (Opens and closes door angrily)
Class: Noisily!
Mimer: (Shakes his head)
Class: Walk to the teacher's desk.
Mimer: (Walks angrily)
Class: Quickly!
Mimer: (Shakes his head)

Variation 2   *Jobs and questions*
One learner mimes a job. The others try to find out what it is by asking not more than twenty questions. The mimer may only shake or nod his head.

Variation 3   *Present continuous*
One learner mimes a sequence of actions. The others try to guess what he is doing. The learner who is miming must nod or shake his head as the class make their guesses, e.g.
Class: You're carrying something.
Mimer: (Nods)
Class: Is it a gun?
Mimer: (Shakes head)
Class: Is it a stick?
Mimer: (Nods)
Class: You're climbing on to something.

Variation 4   *Present perfect*
One learner mimes an action which implies that something else has happened. The others try to guess what it is, e.g.
Mimer: (Holds his thumb with an expression of pain)
Class: Have you hurt your thumb?
Mimer: (Nods head)
Class: Have you hit it?
Mimer: (Nods head)
Class: Have you hit it with a hammer?
Mimer: (Shakes head)

61 What can you do with it?

Language, topic, type of communication	Explaining the possible uses of objects, e.g. *You can put things in it*, or, more tentatively, *I suppose you could . . .*
Skills	Listening and speaking
Degree of control	Guided
Level	Intermediate
Time	10–15 minutes
Preparation	A list of questions (see below). You might like to illustrate these with pictures from magazines. Pictures would stimulate the imagination of the learners but are not essential.
Procedure	Class work

Write a list of objects on the board or OHP, e.g. a paper bag, a hammer, a pram, an empty tin can, a mirror, a table. Display the pictures if you have them. Ask, e.g.

Teacher: How can you use a paper bag?
Learner 1: You can put things in it.
Teacher: Yes, what else can you do with a paper bag?
Learner 2: You can light a fire with it.
Teacher: Yes. Anything else?
Learner 3: You can blow in it and then make a bang!
Learner 4: You could make it into a ball and throw it at someone to attract their attention!

62 Put it together

Language, topic, type of communication	Reading given texts; putting their component parts in correct order.
Skills	Reading, and listening in the Variation
Degree of control	Teacher-controlled
Level	Intermediate/advanced

Time	10–20 minutes, Variation 20–30 minutes.

Preparation   Find some short articles in magazines, newspapers or books which will interest your learners. Cut them up into rectangles. (As the aim is to put the pieces together again you must not cut the pieces in an irregular way because this will help the learners too much!) You may prefer to cut up photocopies of the texts.
Interest is added if you choose illustrated articles.
Keep each article in a separate envelope.
For your own record you might retain a complete photocopy of the article before cutting it up.
(The game can be graded in difficulty by a) the text you choose; b) the number of pieces you cut the text into; c) the degree to which pictures help to give the meaning of the text.)

Procedure   Pair or individual work

Give out the envelopes and ask the learners to read each of the pieces and then place them together in the correct order. The learners should ask you to check that the order is correct.

Variation   Group work
The text here should be a definite story, cut up into strips. A strip is given to each learner in the group, who sit in a circle. Each learner reads out his or her piece of paper, and then they have a general discussion to work out the correct order of the story. They change chairs to sit in the right order and read the whole thing out as the original story.

63   Predicaments

Language, topic, type of communication   Questions and answers about possible future actions, using the formula *What would you do if . . .? I'd . . .*

Skills   Speaking and listening

Degree of control   Guided

Level   Intermediate/advanced

Time   10–15 minutes

Preparation   None

Procedure   Class work

One player leaves the room and the others think of a predicament, e.g. running out of petrol in the middle of the country or in a no-parking area in town; the school burning down; losing all one's money.

The player who went out returns and asks the others in turn: 'What would you do if this happened to you?' Each player must give a reasonable answer, in relation to the predicament which has been agreed. The player whose answer finally reveals the predicament to the questioner can go out next.

64   What's in his pocket?

Language, topic, *type of* *communication*   Describing people, actions, etc. on the basis of given evidence, and giving reasons. Degrees of certainty and uncertainty may be expressed.

Skills   Speaking and writing

Degree of control   Guided

Level   Advanced

Time   30–60 minutes

Preparation   Collect *any* objects which could be carried in someone's pockets, particularly objects collected on a journey or on an evening out. Put a selection of about 15 of the objects in an envelope.
Make up one envelope for each group, or display the 15 objects where everyone can see them.
You can always ask the learners to help you to make a collection of such objects.
Here is an example (it was made at the end of a journey overseas):

1 Air ticket Manchester–Copenhagen–Oslo.
2 Travel agency receipt.
3 Various exchange slips from banks.
4 A small brown paper bag from China.
5 An envelope addressed to Norway with the stamp torn off.
6 A postcard of the mermaid in Copenhagen, stamped but unused.
7 A list of 16 strangely assorted objects.
8 A scrap of paper with 'petrol £5' written on it.
9 Two tickets for an art gallery.

10 A beer mat with a name and number on it.

Procedure   Group work

The aim of the game is to behave like detectives, trying to
understand who the objects belong to, who the person is, what his
interests are, where he has been, what he has done, whom he has
met, etc.
A full and written account should be made.
The source of evidence for each claim should be given, e.g.
Mr A. Wright, who lives at 12 Belfield Road, Manchester 20
OBH, bought an air ticket from Delta Travel Agency,
Manchester, on 12 July 1979. The ticket was for a flight from
Manchester to Oslo via Copenhagen. While he was in Norway he
met someone who had been to China. (The bag appears to be
genuinely from China), etc.
If all groups refer to the same objects, the written accounts may be
compared and displayed.

Summary of the games

Games	Skills	Degree of control	Level	Time in mins	Organisation	Prep.	Page
TRUE/FALSE GAMES							
1 Repeat it if it's true	Listening Speaking	Controlled	Beginners	5–10	Class	Yes	13
2 Correct me if I'm wrong	Listening Speaking Reading	Guided	All	10	Class, group or pair	Yes	14
3 Don't let them pull your leg	Listening Speaking Writing	Free	All	15–20	Class, group or pair	Yes	14
GUESSING GAMES							
4 Hiding and finding	Listening Speaking	Guided	Beginners	15	Class	None	16
5 Box	Listening Speaking	Free	All	5	Class	Yes	17

Games	Skills	Degree of control	Level	Time in mins	Organisation	Prep.	Page
6 What on earth is he talking about?	Listening Speaking Reading Writing	Free	All	10–20	Class, group or pair	Yes	18
MEMORY GAMES							
7 What's behind you?	Listening Speaking	Free	Beginners/ Intermediate	2–3	Class	None	20
8 Kim's game	Listening Speaking Writing	Guided	Beginners/ intermediate	5	Class, optional pair	Yes	21
9 Pass the message	Listening Speaking Reading Writing	Controlled	All	10–30	Class	Yes	23
10 Pelmanism	Listening Speaking Reading	Guided	All	10–15	Group	Yes	25
Variation 1	Listening Speaking	Guided	All	20	Individual or pair and group	Yes	
Variation 2	Reading	Guided	Beginners/ intermediate	5–10	Class	Yes	

QUESTION AND ANSWER GAMES

11	Don't say 'Yes' or 'No'	Listening Speaking	Guided	Intermediate/advanced	5–10	Class, group or pair	None	27
12	Half the class knows	Listening Speaking	Free	All	5–10	Class, group or pair	Yes	28
13	Test your knowledge	Reading	Controlled	Intermediate/advanced	10–20	Pair or individual	Yes	30
14	Twenty questions	Listening Speaking	Free	Intermediate/advanced	15	Class	None	31
15	General knowledge quiz	Listening Speaking	Free	Intermediate/advanced	10–15	Class	Yes	32
16	What were you doing last night?	Listening Speaking	Free	Intermediate/advanced	10–15	Class	None	34

PICTURE GAMES

17	Guess what I'm drawing	Listening Speaking	Guided	Beginners	15–25	Class, pair	Yes	36
18	Copy a picture	Listening Speaking	Guided	Beginners	10–15	Class, pair	Yes	37
19	That's an unusual view!	Listening Speaking	Guided	Beginners	10–15	Class, optional group	Yes	39

Games	Skills	Degree of control	Level	Time in mins	Organisation	Prep.	Page
20 Predicting pictures	Listening Speaking	Guided	Beginners/intermediate	10–15	Class, group or pair	Yes	39
21 Happy twins	Listening Speaking	Free	Intermediate	10–15	Pair	Yes	40
22 Describe a picture	Listening Speaking	Free	Intermediate/advanced	15–20	Pair	Yes	41
Variation	*Listening Speaking Reading Writing*	*Free*	*Intermediate/advanced*	*15–20*	*Pair*	*Yes*	
23 What's the difference?	Listening Speaking	Free	Intermediate/advanced	5–15	Pair	Yes	43
24 Drawing blind	Listening Speaking	Free	Intermediate/advanced	5–10	Class	Yes	45
25 Are you a good detective?	Listening Speaking Reading Writing	Guided	Intermediate/advanced	20–40	Class	Yes	47
26 Super sleuth	Listening Speaking Reading	Guided	Intermediate/advanced	20–30	Class	Yes	47

No.	Title	Skills	Type	Level	Time	Organization	Preparation	Page
27	Would you make a good witness?	Listening Speaking	Free	Intermediate/advanced	10–15	Class	Yes	48
28	Arrange the pictures	Listening Speaking	Free	Intermediate/advanced	5–15	Pair	Yes	50
29	Who are you?	Listening Speaking Reading Writing	Free	Intermediate/advanced	60–80	Individual, class and pair	Yes	51
30	Picture out of focus	Listening Speaking	Free	Intermediate/advanced	10–15	Class	Yes	52
SOUND GAMES								
31	Voices and objects	Listening Speaking	Guided	Beginners	5–10	Class	Yes	53
32	Actions by one person	Listening Speaking	Guided	Beginners	10–15	Class	Yes	54
33	Listening to sounds	Listening Speaking	Guided	Beginners/intermediate	5–10	Class	None	55
34	Actions by more than two people	Listening Speaking	Guided	Intermediate	10–15	Class	Yes	55
35	Using the tape recorder	Listening Speaking	Guided	Intermediate/advanced	20–30	Class or group	Yes	57

Games	Skills	Degree of control	Level	Time in mins	Organisation	Prep.	Page
WORD GAMES							
36 The odd man out	Listening Speaking Reading Writing	Guided	Intermediate	10	Class	Yes	59
Variation	*Listening Speaking Reading Writing*	*Guided*	*Advanced*	*10*	*Group or pair*	*Yes*	
37 Connections	Listening Speaking	Guided	Intermediate/ advanced	5–10	Class, group or pair	None	61
38 Definitions	Listening Speaking	Guided	Advanced	10–15	Class leading to pair	None	61
STORY GAMES							
39 Silly stories	Listening Speaking	Free	Intermediate/ advanced	5–10	Class	None	63
40 Fantasy stories	Listening Speaking Reading Writing	Free	Intermediate/ advanced	30	Group or pair leading to class	Yes	64
41 Alibis	Listening Speaking	Free	Intermediate/ advanced	40–5	Pair leading to class	None	65

No.	Name	Skills	Control	Level	Time	Organization	Prep	Page
42	Confabulation	Listening Speaking Writing	Free	Advanced	30–40	Group or pair leading to class	None	66

PARTY GAMES

No.	Name	Skills	Control	Level	Time	Organization	Prep	Page
43	Kaboom	Listening Speaking	Controlled	Beginners	22–3	Class leading to pair	Yes	67
44	The matchbox	Listening Speaking	Controlled	Beginners	23–5	Class leading to pair	Yes	68
45	Fortune Teller	Listening Speaking Reading Writing	Guided	Beginners	30–40	Class leading to pair	Yes	69
46	Climbing through a postcard	Listening Speaking	Controlled	Beginners/ intermediate	22–3	Class leading to pair	Yes	71
47	The piece of string	Listening Speaking Reading	Controlled	Beginners/ intermediate	22–3	Class leading to pair	Yes	72
48	Consequences	Listening Speaking Reading Writing	Guided	Intermediate	10	Group leading to class	Yes	73
49	Palmistry	Listening Speaking	Free	Advanced	30–60	Class	Yes	75

Games	Skills	Degree of control	Level	Time in mins	Organisation	Prep.	Page
PSYCHOLOGY GAMES							
50 Telepathy	Listening Reading	Controlled	Beginners	10–15	Class	Yes	77
51 Visual perception of length	Listening Speaking	Guided	Beginners	22–3	Class leading to pair	Yes	78
52 The old woman and the young woman	Listening Speaking	Guided	Beginners	5–10	Class	Yes	79
53 Blobs	Listening Speaking	Guided	Beginners/ intermediate	15–30	Class leading to pair	Yes	81
Variation	*Listening Speaking*	*Free*	*Advanced*	*15–30*	*Class*	*Yes*	
54 How quickly can you see?	Listening Speaking	Guided	All	5–10	Class leading to pair	Yes	82
55 Faces and character	Listening Speaking	Free	Intermediate/ advanced	5	Class leading to pair	Yes	83
56 Visual imagery	Speaking and/or Writing	Free	Advanced	5–10	Class	None	84
BINGO GAMES							
57 Number bingo	Listening Speaking Reading Writing	Controlled	Beginners	10–20	Class	Yes	85

Variation 2	Listening Speaking Reading Writing	Controlled	Beginners/ intermediate	10–20	Class	Yes	
MISCELLANEOUS GAMES							
58 Zip	Listening Speaking	Controlled	Beginners	5–10	Class or group	None	87
59 Bumps under the cloth	Listening Speaking	Guided	Beginners/ intermediate	12–13	Class leading to optional pair	Yes	88
Variation	*Listening Speaking*	*Guided*	*Advanced*	*12–13*	*Class*	*Yes*	
60 One idea at a time	Listening Speaking	Guided	Beginners/ intermediate	10–15	Class	None	89
61 What can you do with it?	Listening Speaking	Guided	Intermediate	10–15	Class	Yes	91
62 Put it together	Reading	Controlled	Intermediate/ advanced	10–20	Pair or individual	Yes	91
Variation	*Reading Listening*	*Controlled*	*Intermediate/ advanced*	*20–30*	*Group*	*Yes*	
63 Predicaments	Listening Speaking	Guided	Intermediate/ advanced	10–15	Class	None	92
64 What's in his pocket?	Speaking Writing	Guided	Advanced	30–60	Group	Yes	93

Index

Language

Only the major language items and their principal occurrences are listed here. In organising and playing the games, you will find that unlisted, perhaps unpredictable language items will be required. (The numbers given below refer to the games, *not* the pages.)

Topics

Only the major topics touched on in the games and their principal
occurrences are listed here. (The numbers given below refer to the
games, *not* the pages.)

Types of communication

Only the principal occurrences of the more easily distinguished types of communication are listed here. In organising and playing the majority of games, you will find that unlisted, perhaps unpredictable types of communication will be required. (The numbers given below refer to the games, *not* the pages.)

ASKING QUESTIONS 4 11 12 13 14 15 16 17 22 23 29 31 37 38 41 44 45 48 59 60 63 64

COMPARING 8 22 23 24 51

CORRECTING AND CRITICISING 2 3 18 22 24

DESCRIBING AND NAMING 5 6 7 8 19 21 23 27 28 31 32 33 34 35 43 46 49 51 52 55

EXPRESSING AGREEMENT 10 15 36

EXPRESSING DISAGREEMENT 10 15 36

EXPRESSING DOUBT, UNCERTAINTY, SPECULATION 11 15 30 33 35 51 55 59 62

GIVING ANSWERS 4 11 12 13 14 15 17 22 23 27 29 31 36 37 38 41 44 45 48 59 63 64

GIVING DEFINITIONS 38

GIVING INSTRUCTIONS 24 28

GIVING REASONS 36 37

IDENTIFYING MISTAKES 1 2 3 25 26

INTERRUPTING 2

MAKING PROMISES 61

MAKING SUGGESTIONS 4

NARRATING 32 34 35 39 40 41 42 48